Hope and Healing
for the Abused

Ellel Ministries' Vision Statement

Our Vision

Ellel Ministries is a non-denominational Christian mission organization with a vision to resource and equip the Church by welcoming people, teaching them about the Kingdom of God and healing those in need (Luke 9:11).

Our Mission

Our mission is to fulfill the above vision throughout the world, as God opens the doors, in accordance with the Great Commission of Jesus and the calling of the Church to proclaim the Kingdom of God by preaching the good news, healing the broken-hearted and setting the captives free. We are, therefore, committed to evangelism, healing, deliverance, discipleship and training. The particular scriptures on which our mission is founded are Isaiah 61:1–7, Luke 9:1–2, Luke 9:11, Matthew 28:18–20, Ephesians 4:12 and 2 Timothy 2:2.

Our Basis of Faith

God is a Trinity. God the Father loves all people. God the Son, Jesus Christ, is Savior and Healer, Lord and King. God the Holy Spirit indwells Christians and imparts the dynamic power by which they are enabled to continue Christ's ministry. The Bible is the divinely inspired authority in matters of faith, doctrine and conduct, and is the basis for teaching.

THE TRUTH AND FREEDOM SERIES

Hope and Healing for the Abused

Paul and Liz Griffin

Sovereign World

Sovereign World Ltd
PO Box 784
Ellel
Lancaster LA1 9DA
England

Unless otherwise stated, all scripture quotations are taken from the New International Version. Copyright © 1973, 1978, 1984 by International Bible Society.

NKJV – New King James Version, copyright © 1983, 1992 by Thomas Nelson, Inc.

ISBN: 978 1 85240 480 2

The publishers aim to produce books which will help to extend and build up the Kingdom of God. We do not necessarily agree with every view expressed by the authors, or with every interpretation of Scripture expressed. We expect readers to make their own judgment in the light of their understanding of God's Word and in an attitude of Christian love and fellowship.

All the examples used in this book are real, but names and incidental details have been altered to preserve the privacy of the individuals involved.

Cover design by Andy Taylor, Ellel Ministries
Typeset by CRB Associates, Reedham, Norfolk
Printed in Malta

About the Authors

For twenty years Paul and Liz lived as expatriates in South Africa, Bahrain and Japan. While Paul pursued his career as a chemical engineer with an international oil company, Liz, who trained as a primary school teacher, was a full-time mother bringing up their two children as well as being involved in many Christian activities and a volunteer telephone counseling service. A growing desire to serve the Lord led Paul to resign his job and enroll for a three-year Bible College course back in England. They became involved with Ellel Ministries in 1991 as part of the ministry team. They joined the full-time team at Ellel Grange in 1995. Paul is a member of the Executive Leadership team, and both Paul and Liz teach and minister to those seeking healing in their lives.

Also by the authors:

Anger . . . How Do You Handle It?

Contents

Contents

Foreword

I will never forget the day when I first prayed with a person who had been abused. There have been many critical steps in the development of the vision that resulted in the work of Ellel Ministries, but for me this was one of the most significant.

I had been asked to help a very distressed lady – a lady whose distress I discovered had its origins in sexual abuse. At the time I was ignorant of the extent of abuse, of any sort, that there is in society, both to men and women. I was even more ignorant of the depths of pain caused to those who suffer in this way. And I was shocked to discover that this was also a serious problem inside the Church.

Over thirty years have passed since I was first made aware of the problem. And during that period of time we have been privileged to learn many keys which can open the door to freedom and healing. For some, even healing is a hard path to tread as they have wrestled with the issues of forgiveness. I have wept with those who have been taken advantage of by people they thought could be trusted. At times I have shared their anger at the consequences of what others have done.

In the midst of it all, however, we have seen and experienced the hand of God reaching out to those who are suffering in the most beautiful, and sometimes extraordinary, of ways. Jesus does come to heal the broken-hearted. His compassion knows no limits. Some of those people who trod this path to healing have become dynamic for God in their lives and ministries, as they have lived the reality of knowing that Jesus really does heal today!

I pray that as you read Paul and Liz Griffin's really helpful book, arising from many years' experience helping abused people, that you will begin to understand why, for those who have suffered in this way, life at times seems like a battlefield. The steps to freedom are keys that will help past victims of abuse along the road to deep and lasting healing and be valuable tools for those seeking to help others.

May this book be a real blessing as you find encouragement and hope on the pathway to healing – for yourself and others.

Peter Horrobin
International Director of Ellel Ministries

Preface

We sat patiently watching and waiting as Margaret, the young lady sitting opposite us, restlessly twisted a handkerchief between her fingers. Her head was bowed down and she hardly ever made eye contact with us. Long silences punctuated her conversation but she seemed unaware of this.

For her to say anything at all was difficult. She had never told her story to anyone before and we were relative strangers, whom she'd only met the previous evening. She was struggling to decide whether she could trust us or not. Would this couple listen to her story and then reject her if she told them what she had done? Most of the people in her life, whom she had trusted in the past, had turned out to be untrustworthy and failed her in one way or another.

Margaret had loved and trusted her grandfather until he started touching her inappropriately when she was seven years old. It was just a game he said – something that was a secret between the two of them that no one else must ever know about or she would be punished by being sent away from home. She felt confused because she liked the attention he lavished upon her, but knew deep inside that something was wrong in what they were doing together.

When she was fourteen she discovered she was pregnant but she daren't say anything to her mother. She didn't know whether she would believe her. Even if she did, it would break

Mum's heart to find out what her father had done to his own granddaughter.

Grandfather paid for her to have an abortion, but she had to tell the doctor that she had been sleeping with a boyfriend who had broken up with her the moment she found out that she was pregnant. Not only did she feel furious at the injustice of it, but the guilt of having had the abortion just added to all the other guilt and shame that she was forced to carry.

Margaret had been abused over a period of years and the consequences of this had deeply affected every part of her being. She felt valueless and hated herself. She had often thought of committing suicide. She couldn't trust anyone and, for her, God seemed a long way away.

She had few friends and great difficulty in forming relationships. To the outsider she appeared a shy, quiet person who perhaps just preferred her own company. On the inside, however, there was turmoil and confusion – a mixture of thoughts and emotions that Margaret couldn't easily identify or verbalize, but which held her captive in a life without peace.

Margaret's story is not unusual. Similar struggles to the ones she experienced are faced by many others who have been the victim of abuse. The abuse may not have been over such a long period as Margaret's. The abuse may have been in the form of spiritual manipulation or physical abuse. It may have been mental abuse or emotional abuse or verbal abuse. Many of the consequences, however, will be similar to those that Margaret experienced.

When we first started to pray and minister to people at Ellel Ministries, we were surprised at how many of them had been subjected to some form of abuse in their life. We are now no longer surprised. We may see happy and apparently trouble-free faces each week when we go to church, but many of the people behind those faces could tell us stories of abuse. They have experiences which they are trying to forget or don't want to talk about but which, nevertheless, still influence their lives and hold them back from living the abundant life that Jesus came to bring.

It is for all of these people that we have written this book, to share the truths that God has shown us at Ellel Ministries. We trust that this book will encourage those who have been abused in any way at all to know that Jesus wants to bring healing into their lives.

> *The Spirit of the Sovereign LORD is on me,*
> *because the LORD has anointed me*
> *to preach good news to the poor.*
> *He has sent me to bind up the broken-hearted,*
> *to proclaim freedom for the captives*
> *and release from darkness for the prisoners,*
> *to proclaim the year of the LORD's favour*
> *and the day of vengeance of our God,*
> *to comfort all who mourn,*
> *and provide for those who grieve in Zion –*
> *to bestow on them a crown of beauty*
> *instead of ashes,*
> *the oil of gladness*
> *instead of mourning,*
> *and a garment of praise*
> *instead of a spirit of despair.*
>
> (Isaiah 61:1–3)

We trust that this book will bring understanding where there is confusion and freedom for those in captivity to the past. We pray that it will bring peace where there is turmoil, hope where there is despair, and healing for the oppressed and broken-hearted.

Paul and Liz Griffin
January 2007

Not as God Intended

Open any daily newspaper today and the headlines will proclaim the real-life stories of abuse from around the world and from all strata of society – stories of child-trafficking in the Far East, abuse of prisoners in detention camps, wanton violence by drunken football fans, patients in psychiatric wards being sexually molested, fraudulent charity collectors deceiving old age pensioners, and even ministers of religion involved in sordid sex scandals with vulnerable members of their congregations.

It is abundantly clear that we live in a society in which the way individuals treat one another is not as God intended. Instead we live in a society in which self-glorification and self-gratification are rampant driving forces in the lives of many. Such people selfishly satisfy their own desires, indifferent to the pain and heartbreak they inflict upon others.

We live in a society in which physical, emotional, verbal, spiritual, racial and sexual abuse is seldom out of the news. This society is reflected in the stories of those whom we have counseled and prayed with over the years.

How do you define abuse?

We define abuse as the wrong or improper use of something or someone. It involves using others without their consent or understanding, for our own purposes. It is to treat another person as a thing rather than as a person. It is to ridicule, shame, or damage that other person by our words or actions.

Abuse involves the wrong use of relationships. It means disregarding others' basic right to be treated with dignity. Abuse overrides free will and ignores the fact that others are trying to say "no." It manipulates them until they feel they have no choice but to say "yes."

This is how one lady put it into words as she shared publicly on a training course at one of our centers: "My boundaries were mown down by people when I was little. As a result I've been too passive all my life and I've suffered from chronic fatigue syndrome for years. I've realized now that I must be active in my healing and deny the enemy any foothold in my life. I feel very excited about what I've learnt on this course."

We pray with many who have been used wrongly, taken advantage of, or betrayed. In this book we want to explore some of the ways this has happened and offer hope and steps to healing to all those who have suffered abuse in any way.

The first few chapters describe some of the huge variety of abuses people may suffer. The next section deals with ways in which we, as human beings, tend to respond to abuse. The later chapters cover what may be happening in the spiritual realm and how Jesus brings hope and healing.

Abuse among family and friends

Abuse can take place among friends. We all have a desire to be accepted and don't like the pain of rejection. The desire to be included can leave us vulnerable to peer pressure. That pressure can result in our being manipulated into doing things we would rather not do. Rather than face rejection or exclusion from the group we may allow our will to be overridden and we may make ungodly choices.

Some people might, for example, choose to join their friends in ridiculing, bullying and abusing someone who has upset another member of the group. To become a member of the group they might even participate in gang initiation ceremonies which include sexually abusive practices.

Abuse can take place in families. It may be sexual abuse of children by parents, step-parents or grandparents. Sometimes such abuse is by older brothers or sisters, cousins or other relatives. Many of those who come for help have experienced some form of sexual abuse from close relatives.

Abuse within the family setting may be through the control or manipulation of a mother-in-law. Sadly, some mothers feel unwilling to really release and let go of their adult children emotionally, even after those sons and daughters have married. As a result they try to control and influence decisions within that marriage and interfere with the right development of a husband and wife's relationship.

Family abuse may be within a marriage relationship itself. One partner may begin manipulation by granting or with-holding sexual favors. Such behavior distorts the beautiful gift of intimacy that God has given to be enjoyed freely and unconditionally within the marriage relationship.

Very commonly in families there is physical abuse because of unfair discipline or a parent lashing out at a child in anger. In other families domestic violence takes place between husbands and wives. Such aggressive behavior accounts for nearly 20 percent of all violent crime reported in the UK. Half of all murders of women in the UK are committed by their male partner, usually after a long period of domestic violence.

Abuse in the workplace

For some, the workplace is a place of abuse. Countless documentaries force us to recognize that children are exploited in third world countries. Children as young as five or six have little choice but to work long hours for a pittance, in order to be able to buy enough food to survive for yet another day of abject poverty and misery.

Thankfully, industrial legislation has helped to eliminate such abuses in the "more developed" countries. However, even in these countries, employers can still place unfair pressure and expectations on their employees. Bosses are abusing their employees when they deliberately choose not to give affirmation for a job well done or presume upon people's loyalty in an unreasonable way and fail to give them any free-will choices.

Age, gender or race have been the basis for discrimination or abuse in the workplace. For some it may have been open and obvious in the words that were spoken. For others, it may have been the experience of knowing that they have been unfairly passed over for promotion or treated differently from their peers at work, without any explanation having been given.

Many women have experienced sexual harassment or had to endure sexual innuendo from their male colleagues. Fearful of the consequences of confronting such behavior, they have suffered in silence, suppressing their anger and pain at the treatment they had to endure.

Abuse in institutions

Instead of being places of healing, the health services and hospitals may also be places of damage. Patients have sometimes been treated with a lack of respect and dignity – treated as a case rather than a person. They may have been denied privacy or been made to feel that they were a nuisance.

We read of cases where vulnerable elderly patients have been neglected instead of receiving the care and attention they desperately need. Tragically, some who were unable to feed themselves have even been left to starve.

We hear of abuse of prisoners by staff and fellow prisoners. Wardens have authority and power and can misuse it. They can discriminate against a particular prisoner and make their time in jail as miserable as possible. They can fail to protect those under their care. By turning a blind eye they can allow prisoners to be bullied and physically or sexually abused. Homosexual rape is a real fear for many male prisoners.

Within the military and similar organizations such as the police force, the authority structure is open to misuse. There have been incidents of bullying, public humiliation and shaming of new recruits. Training aimed at conditioning recruits to submit to orders without question can cease being a rightful form of order and control and can cross the boundaries of acceptable behavior.

Abuse in the church

Throughout the Bible we see that good leadership is essential in God's kingdom. We rejoice in what God is doing in the body of Christ and the many leaders who are answering God's call to serve Him in full-time ministry. Our churches need to be places of safety and security where godly leaders know how to use their authority in the right way.

Sadly, this isn't always the case. Some people reluctantly share that they have felt controlled or manipulated by pastors or house-group leaders. Because they don't wish to be wrongfully judgmental of those whom God has called and anointed, they have often struggled with the pain and guilt of sharing what has happened to them. We have heard how people have courageously tried to confront the issues only to be made to feel that they are not submissive but rebellious.

Having said that, we fully recognize that the majority of pastors and leaders are doing their best to be the leaders God wants them to be, sometimes under very difficult circumstances. We have heard from pastors who suffer great pain because they are placed under unfair pressure or unreasonable expectations by congregations. They are expected to be always available and to put the needs of their congregations above the needs of their own spouses and children.

Abuse in school

Some people have experienced abuse at school. When I (Paul) was at school nearly fifty years ago, abuse in schools was likely to be the excessive use of corporal punishment by teachers. In the school I attended, the teachers all had leather straps which they were very quick to use for any misdemeanor. I can remember a day when students, who had an hour's bus ride to school, were punished for being late for assembly on a morning when a thick fog meant that all the traffic was moving slowly and delays were inevitable.

Such physical abuse is less common nowadays but teachers can still maltreat students by publicly shaming or ridiculing them. These days they might not put a dunce's hat on their head and make them stand in front of the whole class, as happened to one lady we prayed with. But they might cause just as much pain with sarcastic comments or by dismissing with disdain the hard work of a student attempting to do his or her best.

Such treatment can have devastating results. David, who came to Ellel Grange recently, told us his experiences: "God showed me the damage done by emotional, mental and physical abuse when I was at boarding school, aged six. I had to forgive and be released from bitterness, hatred, anger, resentment and fear. I had learned then to fight my way through life and I've been doing that ever since. Now my personality can be at ease and receive God's love, acceptance and peace in the way it ought to be – very precious!"

With the breakdown of family life and an increasing number of unhappy children growing up in broken homes, it's not uncommon now to read of students verbally or even physically abusing their teachers. A short time ago there was even a case of a student on trial for raping his teacher.

In recent years there seems to have been an increase in the incidents of bullying among pupils in schools and a greater awareness of the problem. For some of the people we pray with, such experiences meant that their schooldays were far from being "the happiest days of their lives." How tragic it is to open a newspaper and read of a teenager's suicide note explaining their action by saying that they could no longer endure the bullying of their classmates.

Abuse by the media

We can be abused by the media. Visual images that we would rather not see can suddenly be there in our homes as we watch television. As viewers we can feel slimed or defiled by the language or content of a program.

Some people have had their character assassinated by reports based on slander and lies. Interviews are edited and presented in a way that distorts the truth. The media can become both the judge and jury with the victims of such character defamation being given little or no right to reply and defend themselves.

The media have great power in determining what is, or is not, newsworthy. By careful selection they can mold public opinion. I recently saw a program maker advertising for people who had had a bad experience of Christian healing to contact them. How sad and unbalanced that the advert did not also ask for people with a positive testimony to contact them.

With unbalanced reporting we can feel that public opinion has been carefully manipulated. Issues and values that are important to us can be unfairly presented or attacked and as a result we can feel a sense of abuse.

Summary

In this first chapter we have been looking at what we mean by abuse and how we can encounter it. You may perhaps recognize that you have been abused in one way or another or that you have abused others. God knows the details of every circumstance in our lives and, through Jesus, has made provision for cleansing and healing from all the abuse we have experienced.

In the next chapter we will explore in more detail issues relating to verbal abuse.

The Power of Words

How do you feel when someone says something that builds you up or encourages you? How do you feel when someone tells you that you look good or that you have done a good job or that you have helped them or blessed them? The answer for nearly all of us is that we feel good on the inside when we are blessed in this way. That's the way God planned it to be.

God has created us as relational beings. He has created us to relate to Himself and to relate to one another. God's perfect plan for our lives is that we should bless one another through our actions and through our words.

Blessing or cursing

There are many scriptures that tell us of the importance of encouraging each other with our words. For example:

> An anxious heart weighs a man down,
>   but a kind word cheers him up.

(Proverbs 12:25)

> A word aptly spoken
>   is like apples of gold in settings of silver.

(Proverbs 25:11)

Pleasant words are a honeycomb,
  sweet to the soul and healing to the bones.

(Proverbs 16:24)

We can use our words to bless one another but we can also use them to abuse or curse one another. Satan wants us to use our tongue to destroy and not to encourage, to reject and not to accept, to denigrate and not to affirm. There is great power in the words that we speak out.

Our words have the power to pull down and destroy or the power to build up and encourage.

Reckless words pierce like a sword,
  but the tongue of the wise brings healing.

(Proverbs 12:18)

The tongue has the power of life and death,
  and those who love it will eat its fruit.

(Proverbs 18:21)

The good man brings good things out of the good stored up in his heart, and the evil man brings evil things out of the evil stored up in his heart. For out of the overflow of his heart his mouth speaks.

(Luke 6:45)

With the tongue we praise our Lord and Father, and with it we curse men, who have been made in God's likeness.

(James 3:9)

Verbal abuse

Verbal abuse can be defined as the use of words to bring emotional hurt or cursing into someone's life. It is using words to shame, ridicule and belittle another. It is speaking lies and false accusations against others in a way that demeans them and fails to give them respect.

The damage caused by these words depends upon how close the relationship is between the person speaking the words and the one receiving them. The closer the relationship, the more damaging the words can be. If a mother says to her child, "I hate you," it will cause far more damage than those same words spoken by another child in the school playground during a squabble.

The tone and manner in which words are spoken significantly increases the damage. Looking someone in the eyes and speaking out words slowly and with venom will penetrate into a person's soul and spirit far more deeply than the same words spoken casually or in a moment of anger.

Warnings from Jesus

Jesus Himself told us we must be very careful about the words we speak to one another. He even likened the use of certain words to an act of murder.

> *"You have heard that it was said to the people long ago, 'Do not murder, and anyone who murders will be subject to judgment.' But I tell you that anyone who is angry with his brother will be subject to judgment. Again, anyone who says to his brother, 'Raca,' is answerable to the Sanhedrin. But anyone who says, 'You fool!' will be in danger of the fire of hell."*
> (Matthew 5:21–22)

Jesus recognized that the enemy loves to use our words to bring discouragement to others. When Peter, one of His closest friends, was rebuking Jesus for saying that He would have to go to Jerusalem and be put to death, Jesus turned to Peter and said those oft-quoted words:

*"Get behind me, Satan! You are a stumbling-block to me; you
do not have in mind the things of God, but the things of men."*

(Matthew 16:23)

Only moments earlier Jesus had been praising Peter for declaring
that He was the Messiah – "the Anointed One of God." How
easy it is for us to identify with Peter. One moment we are
speaking out words that please God and the next our words
are the mouthpiece for the enemy.

Abusive words which are spoken can reflect the true attitude
of someone's heart. They expose the inner thoughts and
attitudes. If we receive such words we can find them painful
and damaging. They suddenly strip away all security we
thought we had in our relationship with the speaker, leaving
us shocked, vulnerable or confused.

Words of accusation and condemnation

When we are falsely accused of something, this is also verbal
abuse. Have you ever been attacked like this when you were
innocent: "It's all your fault"; "You are to blame"; "You did
it"; "You stole it"; "You're wicked"; "You're a liar"; "You're a
harlot"? These false words are an attack upon our integrity and
our character. They imply that we acted out of a malicious
heart. Such words penetrate into our spirit and crush us.

Words that condemn us are also abusive. We may have had
people say such things to us as: "You ought to be punished";
"You should suffer for what you've done"; "You're not fit to
live with decent people and I hope you rot in hell"; "Somebody
ought to shoot you"; "You will end up in prison"; "You're just
like your father."

These words of condemnation judge us in an unfavorable
light. They accuse us and pass sentence upon us. If such words
are spoken to us by an adult when we are a child, we will
invariably believe them. We may well develop a belief that we

deserve to be punished and accept all the bad experiences of life as deserved punishment coming from God.

The verbal abuse may be judgmental words of criticism. People may write us off with such statements as: "You're hopeless"; "You're useless"; "You never get things right"; "You're a complete failure"; "You will never amount to anything"; "You will never succeed"; "Nobody will want to marry you"; "Nobody will ever employ you"; "You're just out for yourself."

These judgments are often expressed as black and white statements – they state we *always* or we *never* behave in a particular way. They may highlight a real weakness or mistake in us but claim that such weaknesses or mistakes occur all the time. The words pull down rather than build up and they give us no scope for change.

The words may only be heard once but are not easily forgotten. They replay themselves over and over again in our mind. They come back into our memory to bring turmoil and torment. The lies that have been spoken begin to be accepted as truth and shape the way we see ourselves.

Words that bring death to our spirit

Words that are spoken out of anger can be abusive and damaging. They may be words like: "I hate you"; "I never want to see you again"; "Go away and never come back"; "I wish you were dead"; "I wish I'd never married you"; "I wish you had never been born." Such words are particularly painful when spoken out by someone we love or are dependent upon. They penetrate deep into our spirit bringing death rather than life.

Abusive words bring us despair and doom: "You will never pass the exam"; "You never get anything right"; "You will always be a loser"; or "You are sure to get this disease, it runs in the family."

Such words are pronouncements and curses. If you are the target of such words you may receive and believe them and then the enemy is empowered to make them self-fulfilling. Often we take these pronouncements of others and make them into self-pronouncements: "I will never pass this exam" or "I will always be a loser." We believe our own pronouncements and so we stop trying.

Words can be used in an abusive and sarcastic way to ridicule and mock: "Here comes four-eyes"; "You're not half the man my father was"; "A five-year-old could do it better than that." Words spoken out in this way damage our self-esteem. They are like arrows that penetrate into our spirit.

One lady said that during her childhood her mother often used to say, "I don't know why I bother to ask you to help; I could do it much better myself." These words left her feeling inadequate and unappreciated. Instead of being nourished in her spirit she had been crushed. Believing anything she did would not be good enough, she gave up even trying. Others then criticized her for being lazy and not doing enough to help. The effect of negative words was thus continually being reinforced in her life, becoming a vicious cycle in her life.

Words of curse

Spoken words can act as curses. They are negative words that not only cause deep wounding but can also lock us into whatever has been said. Words of curse establish rights for the enemy to work in our lives.

Even though the words that have been spoken are untrue we start to believe them, especially when they are repeated to us over and over again. Our belief in the false words then empowers the enemy. The words become a foundation where the enemy is able to build a stronghold in our lives. They can act like invisible chains tying us to the person who spoke them.

One lady shared with us that when she finished a relationship with a boyfriend he said, "You'll never be free of me." She said she still felt his presence although they had split up a number of years ago. When we prayed for her and asked God to break all that kept her chained to him spiritually, she had quite a strong physical reaction. Afterwards she found that God had healed her of asthma and she was able to breathe normally. She had suffered from asthma attacks ever since the break-up of the relationship and the words of curse spoken by her ex-boyfriend.

Another person told us how she had been verbally abused by a gipsy who spoke these words to her, "I hope you and your children are handicapped." As she shared her story she told us that, subsequently, two of her children had been born with physical handicaps.

Summary

We can be abused by the words that people speak into our lives. These abusive words cause crushing of our human spirit and can leave us feeling rejected, guilty and confused. Often we underestimate the effect of words and of verbal abuse in our lives. Release from the power of the words of others sets us free to grow and mature in our God-given identity.

In the next chapter we will explore how we can be emotionally controlled and abused when someone manipulates our emotions so that we act according to their desire and agenda.

Emotionally Controlled

Have you ever done something that someone asked you to do because you felt too guilty or embarrassed to say no? Have you ever done something that someone asked you to do because you were fearful of their response if you said no? If you can answer yes to either of these questions you may have been a victim of emotional abuse.

Emotional abuse can be said to occur when a person uses the power of their own emotions (such as anger) in order to stimulate the emotions (such as fear) of another and so causes emotional harm or manipulates them in some way. It is a powerful control mechanism that leaves victims feeling that they have been used and coerced into actions that they feel uncomfortable about.

Emotions motivate our actions

Emotions are the inner reactions or feelings that we have to events or circumstances (real or perceived) in our lives. They are a measure of how we feel about ourselves and our environment.

Our behavior, our thoughts and our emotions are closely interrelated. Our emotions are influenced by our thoughts and the direction of our thoughts is influenced by our emotions. If we feel anxious in our present environment we may well start to think about the negative things that might happen to us. Our thoughts then reinforce the emotion of fear.

Our decisions and actions, including decisions to take no action, primarily spring from our thoughts. In our minds we evaluate the different choices that are open to us. Sometimes this evaluation is almost instantaneous and instinctive. At other times we carefully weigh the options before taking action. As we do this we experience feelings about each of the options. We can say, therefore, that our final choice of action is affected by our emotions. Emotions motivate and energize our actions.

If we feel insecure in a particular situation, our emotion of fear may be influencing us to run away. The more we think about what might happen in this insecure environment, the more fearful we become. The more fearful we become, the stronger will be the desire to run away. Our emotions motivate our actions.

It can be difficult for us to put into words exactly what we are feeling at any one time, as we may be experiencing a mixture of emotions. Our emotions or feelings can be positive or they can be negative. We enjoy the good positive feelings we have when things are going well. We feel pleased with life and full of energy. We feel encouraged, ready for action and willing to face new challenges.

We don't like the unpleasant feelings we experience when things are not going well. We can feel drained of energy and the simplest tasks can seem daunting. We feel discouraged and sometimes depressed. We may feel uncertain and confused as to how we should act. It often seems safer to withdraw and be passive.

One of the reasons why God gave us emotions was because He wanted us to enjoy life. If we had no feelings about the things we do in life, there wouldn't be any incentive to do anything that we enjoy. Our emotions can be a motivating force in our lives. Even negative emotions like grief and sadness about the misfortunes of others, can cause us to want to reach out and help them. Anger at injustice can be a motivating force driving us to alleviate the injustice. The way we feel about something invariably influences the way we behave.

Controlled through fear

We can use our emotions to control or manipulate others in order to achieve our objectives and desires. We can threaten to get angry if others don't do what we want them to do. They become fearful of what might happen if we express our anger. The anger may result in an unpleasant scene or even lead to violence. If there have been previous outbreaks of anger, this will serve to reinforce the fearful response of the victim.

The fear of what might happen if we should be displeased or lose our temper causes our victims to do everything in their power to stop this happening. They will tiptoe around us. They will try to gauge our mood. They will carefully weigh their words before speaking, trying to assess the likely response they will receive from us.

They become submissive to our request and do what they have been asked to do; they make choices for wrong motives. We have effectively taken away their free-will choice and manipulated them to act in the way we want them to behave. We have used our emotions to stimulate the emotions of our victim so that we can control their behavior.

If people have been emotionally abused and controlled in this way, they can become very passive. We have ministered to many who felt controlled by either a mother or a father, and they have also admitted that they were afraid of this parent's anger. The fear that Dad might lose his temper led them to be submissive to his will. Even if Dad sometimes gave them sensible and godly advice, they resented it because inside they felt they had no choice but to submit.

Controlled by guilt

Instead of stimulating the emotion of fear, emotional abuse may consist of using self-pity to induce false guilt in victims and control decisions. We can say such things as, "If you knew how lonely I'll feel, you wouldn't go out and leave me all on my own" or "No one ever invites me to go out to dinner." We can cause such feelings of guilt that people then change their minds about what they were going to do. They might decide not to go out after all or they might invite us to join them in going out to dinner. That might get us what we want, but manipulating someone's emotions is a form of abuse.

Emotional abusers may not be fully aware of what they are doing or they may be cold and calculating, deliberately choosing words in such a way that their own desires are met. Either way victims feel that they have been controlled and dominated and their free will has been overridden.

Summary

In this chapter we have explored how we can use the power of emotions to control others and make them do what we want. We have looked at how it feels to be abused and controlled when someone stimulates our emotions to cause us to behave in the way they want us to. Healing comes through being released from the ungodly control of others and being set free to make the godly choices that Jesus would have us make.

In the next chapter we will explore how we can be spiritually abused when those in spiritual authority over us fail to fulfill their roles as good shepherds of the flock.

Failed by the Shepherds

In this chapter we want to look at what we will call spiritual abuse. We define spiritual abuse as the misuse of spiritual authority or power by one person over another, causing damage to spiritual well-being and hampering spiritual potential. We would say that any actions or words that cause people to have a distorted picture of God's heart and will for their life is a form of spiritual abuse. An alternative definition might be the mistreatment of someone who is in need of help, support or spiritual strengthening.

In any organization with an authority structure there is potential for someone to misuse authority and so abuse others. This is true for business and political organizations, and it is also true within Christian organizations and the church.

Problems today

There are many good and caring leaders within the body of Christ but, sadly, there are also those who, for various reasons, have failed the flock under their care. As we pray with people we hear how some have been hurt and damaged by those in spiritual authority over them.

We realize that sometimes what we hear may only be their perception of what happened. It is only one side of the story.

Nevertheless, those telling us their stories have been scarred and damaged by what they have experienced.

The body of Christ needs godly leadership and authority. Congregations need to respect and honor their leaders and those leaders in turn need to be humble and servant-hearted. As the writer to the letter to the Hebrews tells us, church leaders will have to give an account to God for the care they have exercised over their flocks:

> Obey your leaders and submit to their authority. They keep watch over you as men who must give an account. Obey them so that their work will be a joy, not a burden, for that would be of no advantage to you.
>
> (Hebrews 13:17)

Structure within the church should provide security – security for the church members, knowing that their shepherds are concerned above all else for their welfare; security for the shepherds knowing that they have the respect of their sheep. Unfortunately this is not always so.

Not a new problem

The failure of those with spiritual authority to fulfill the role entrusted to them is not a new problem. In the days of Ezekiel, God rebuked the priests and religious leaders for falling short:

> "This is what the Sovereign LORD says: Woe to the shepherds of Israel who only take care of themselves! Should not shepherds take care of the flock? ... You have not strengthened the weak or healed the sick or bound up the injured. You have not brought back the strays or searched for the lost. You have ruled them harshly and brutally ... I am against the shepherds and will hold them accountable for my flock."
>
> (Ezekiel 34:2, 4, 10)

God expressed His anger at the religious leaders for not looking after the flock. The people had needs but these were not being met. Instead they were being ruled out of a legalistic heart rather than by a heart of compassion.

Jesus rebuked the Pharisees in a similar way for failing to help the people:

> *"The teachers of the law and the Pharisees sit in Moses' seat. So you must obey them and do everything they tell you. But do not do what they do, for they do not practise what they preach. They tie up heavy loads and put them on men's shoulders, but they themselves are not willing to lift a finger to move them."*
>
> (Matthew 23:2–4)

God is looking for church leaders who will act as His under-shepherds and treat the flock under their care as He would. When this doesn't happen, the heart of God is grieved.

> *Jesus went through all the towns and villages, teaching in their synagogues, preaching the good news of the kingdom and healing every disease and sickness. When he saw the crowds, he had compassion on them, because they were harassed and helpless, like sheep without a shepherd.*
>
> (Matthew 9:35–36)

Threats, intimidation and ungodly control

Sadly, when relationships have gone wrong in the church, some leaders have used threats and intimidation to try to impose their will upon people in their congregation and prevent them from leaving. One pastor even told a couple they would lose their salvation if they went. Another said the shocking words, "I damn you and your family to hell."

We have been told of some church leaders who have publicly humiliated members of the congregation, denouncing them as sinners, false prophets or troublemakers. They have told these people to leave the church and instructed everyone in the congregation to cut off all relationships with them. In some extreme circumstances it may be necessary for a pastor to ask someone to leave the church, but it needs to be done with great wisdom and sensitivity.

Other leaders have preached sermons revealing private and confidential matters to the whole congregation. Even if actual names have not been mentioned, it has not been difficult to work out identities. We feel this is a form of abuse because people have placed their trust in a leader when they have confided some of their struggles and problems.

Leaders, in their lack of security, have damaged people by dogmatic assertions which leave no allowance for disagreement. They claim that their opinion is what the Bible teaches and no one is allowed any other interpretation. We do believe there is a need to be dogmatic about foundational Christian truths. But there are issues on which theologians don't all agree and it can be arrogant to insist that everyone who doesn't hold to our own view on such issues is in the wrong.

Some leaders, in their zeal, have exercised too much control over individuals' lives. They have insisted on absolute loyalty to the church and have forbidden members from going elsewhere. One pastor told the congregation that they were not to go to a specific Christian meeting which was outside of the church. He had considered the matter, made up his mind and did not want any further discussion. We recognize that there is a need for leaders to warn and protect their flock from false teaching, but insisting on absolute loyalty to the leader is overstepping the boundary between guidance and control.

Some church leaders have told people whom they should or should not marry. One lady told us how, shortly after her marriage, her house-group leader used to make remarks along the lines of "Haven't you started a family yet?" In fact she felt so pressurized that she stopped taking her contraceptive pills despite the agreement she had with her spouse that they would wait two years following their marriage before having children.

Overriding of free will

People can be spiritually abused when they feel they have to submit to uninvited prayer and ministry. Some have been picked out of the congregation and effectively ordered to the front of the meeting so that the speaker can publicly pray for them. Another speaker went up to one lady in a church service and, without asking if she would like to have prayer, said, "You have a spirit of witchcraft and I'm going to deliver you."

At one meeting we were attending, a guest speaker said to the congregation, "If you want to see a miracle, come and surround this lady in the wheelchair whilst I pray for her." Even though a miracle did not take place the speaker insisted that she was only following the leading of God and had not got it wrong.

Some have been abused through harsh and unfair church discipline or insensitive counseling. People who needed to be listened to because they were hurting and had deep inner healing problems have been dismissed with a curt, "You need to read the Bible more."

A lady whose husband had committed suicide was told by her church leadership: "The church is really struggling to come to terms with this. We think it would be better if you left the church and went somewhere else."

Spiritual abuse takes place when a congregation is controlled or manipulated to make the leader look good. Some examples of this would be: "You should all be coming to the front in response to this message"; "God wants you all to be at the meeting tomorrow night"; and "If you had any faith you would be financially supporting this project."

When spiritual leaders speak such words they create the impression that they are conveying God's view to all those who are listening. Within their spirit, however, many of them may feel uncomfortable with what has been said. They may feel confused or think they are being rebellious in not fully wanting to comply with the request. They may go along with it, driven by false guilt, but knowing that something is not quite right. They may well conclude that it is something within their own heart attitude that is wrong.

Circumstances that may lead to spiritual abuse

There are circumstances within churches which could develop into a breeding ground for spiritual abuse. A leadership structure which is characterized by a strong hierarchical system can create positions of power and authority. Rather than earning the respect of those under them which leads to willing submission, those holding positions of authority can use their position to override people's free will. They try to force submission by saying things like, "I am the music director and what I say, goes." Instead of willing submission and the security of feeling led, individuals feel controlled and driven by their leaders.

Sometimes it can be the insecurity of church leaders that creates the problems. Their own fear of rejection or failure causes them to be controlling and domineering. They want to make the decisions without discussion. If anyone disagrees with them they accuse these people of being troublemakers or in rebellion. If the church is an independent one with no higher authority giving oversight, nobody is there to provide balance. An accused church member cannot appeal to anyone else for resolution of the problem.

It is wonderful to have people in a congregation who are totally committed to serving God, but they can be taken advantage of and exploited by an over-zealous leader. Some may take on more responsibilities than God is asking them to. In their desire to please God they may be reluctant to say "no" to the requests from the church leaders to teach the Sunday School, lead the women's group and run a house group whilst trying to bring up four young children! In their hearts they might conclude that God is a very hard taskmaster.

Abuse of the church leader

It is not only members of congregations who can be the victims of spiritual abuse. Sometimes church leaders themselves can be abused by people in their churches. As human beings they are unable to be perfect and will make mistakes. Rather than being criticized, they really need us to undergird their ministries with our support and prayers. We can fail to give them the respect and honor that should be theirs. Sometimes they are undermined by gossip or someone stirring up dissension amongst the congregation. Have you ever been guilty of attacking your own leader?

In the Bible there is a warning about grumbling against God and spiritual leaders:

> *They travelled from Mount Hor along the route to the Red Sea, to go round Edom. But the people grew impatient on the way; they spoke against God and against Moses, and said, "Why have you brought us up out of Egypt to die in this desert? There is no bread! There is no water! And we detest this miserable food!"*
>
> *Then the LORD sent venomous snakes among them; they bit the people and many Israelites died. The people came to Moses and said, "We sinned when we spoke against the LORD and against you. Pray that the LORD will take the snakes away from us."*
>
> (Numbers 21:4–7)

When we pray with church leaders we usually ask them if they are happy for us to pray about the words of criticism that any of their congregation has spoken. As we do this, we are often led in the name of Jesus to break the demonic power of anything released through such words. We frequently see manifestations followed by a sense of peace and joy returning to the leader.

Abuse through counterfeit gifts of the Spirit

Congregations and individuals can be manipulated and abused through the operation of counterfeit spiritual gifts. Their origin may be soulish or even demonic but in either case they cause a lot of damage to the church congregation. Great confusion can be caused when false prophecies are endorsed as true.

One such message, which we heard endorsed by a church leader, was, "God is angry with all of you for not attending the midweek prayer meeting." It was true that some needed to be encouraged to attend the prayer meeting, but to say that God was displeased and angry because everyone didn't attend was allowing the enemy to bring in guilt and condemnation. It was not in keeping with what we know of the loving character of Father God and was not a message coming from the Holy Spirit.

Sometimes congregations are manipulated and abused when leaders promote soulish visions which are not of God but which reflect their own desires or agendas. We would call this sort of thing "soulish" because it originates in the person's own mind, will and emotions, rather than from God. Some examples of this would be: "God wants us to believe that He will increase the membership of this church from 10 to 5,000" or, in a church where the average attendance is only 80 people in total, "God is saying that we should be praying for 100 souls to be saved on Sunday night."

Such manipulation and abuse leads people into spiritual confusion, guilt and disillusionment. They may feel that the visions which were supposed to be from God didn't materialize because of their own lack of faith. They may conclude that it is better not to trust what church leaders say and so they withdraw and refuse to submit to godly leadership. They may conclude that God Himself can't be trusted so that any faith they had in Him is destroyed.

The above are examples of extreme spiritual abuse which have been shared with us. In quoting these examples we don't want to give the impression that all those in spiritual authority abuse those under their authority. Most church leaders are sold out for Jesus and want the very best for their flock.

Godly leadership includes the exercising of spiritual authority to bring guidance and correction. The aim of such guidance or discipline is not to build up or enhance the status or position of the leader but for the good of the people that he or she cares about. The apostle Paul summarizes this well in his letter to the Corinthian church:

> *This is why I write these things when I am absent, that when I come I may not have to be harsh in my use of authority – the authority the Lord gave me for building you up, not for tearing you down.*
>
> (2 Corinthians 13:10)

In their zeal to serve God, leaders can easily be misunderstood or they can fail to communicate effectively. If they sometimes make mistakes we need to be careful that we don't wrongly judge the attitude of their hearts. We need to pray for and encourage our leaders, perhaps by using the following simple prayer:

We thank You, God, for all those who have been called to serve as leaders within the body of Christ. We pray that You will bless them and give them wisdom and strength in all that they do. Amen.

Summary

In this chapter we have been looking at the ways in which we can be spiritually abused. Through ungodly control and manipulation we can end up with a distorted concept of how God sees us and what He expects of us. Freedom and release from the confusion and pain of spiritual abuse begins with understanding the true nature of God as our loving heavenly Father.

In the next chapter we will together explore issues relating to physical abuse.

Beaten Inside and Out

Abuse always results in damage on the inside but it can start with damage on the outside. In this chapter we are going to explore together some of the issues relating to physical abuse.

Definition

Physical abuse is the exercise of physical power over another to inflict physical pain or damage. It includes subjecting an individual to harsh and unfair punishment or restraint and wrongly justifying such actions as discipline.

Physical abuse also includes neglect. This neglect is the result of those in authority failing to meet the needs of those under their care and protection. It is failing to provide them with necessary physical attention. Such abuse or neglect might come from parents, guardians or foster parents. It might come from those in positions of responsibility in places such as care homes, hospitals or prisons.

Although physical abuse affects the body we need to recognize that the consequences are much deeper. We are a unity of body, soul and spirit and anything that affects the body can have an effect on the rest of our being. Physical abuse will influence the way we think, the choices we make, our emotional responses, and it will cause crushing and damage to our human spirits.

Domestic violence

There was a couple who explained to us that God had brought them together and told them to marry each other, even though they had hardly known each other for any length of time. They found a verse in the Bible which they said confirmed it, although it didn't seem very clear to us. When they asked the pastor to do the wedding in the church he advised them to wait for six months. Ignoring his counsel they went to another pastor who agreed to do the wedding straight away. Sadly the young woman came back to the first pastor after a few months and said that she was being beaten violently by her husband.

Another couple we knew also decided that God was bringing them together and yet shortly after their marriage we found out they were both being physically violent towards each other. They were arguing over such issues as what kind of food to eat, who was the better driver and what time to go to bed. Whenever he said something which hurt her she would scream and punch him in the face or pull his hair. He would then retaliate by hitting her, justifying it by saying she started the fighting.

The enemy loves to bring disunity and division and he is the winner when marriages turn violent. The victims are generally wives and children, although it is, sadly, quite common for wives to throw crockery or the nearest thing that comes to hand at their husbands. Abuse in the home is often accompanied by alcohol abuse. The alcohol lessens the ability to hold the emotions in check and as a result emotions are expressed in ungodly ways.

We have often heard how women have almost died because men in anger and rage have placed their hands around their throats and tried to strangle them. Such incidents are traumatic and frightening and severely fracture the trust upon which successful marriages depend.

Husbands who have been physically abusive towards their wives and have come for help are truly sorry for what has happened but often express helplessness in knowing how to stop it happening again. Suppressed deep-seated anger from childhood is often the root cause. Their anger comes to the surface, they lose control and they express the anger physically against their spouse.

Victims of domestic violence confess that they can cope more easily with the physical pain than the resultant emotional pain and confusion. They can still love and want the best for their spouse but the loss of trust and respect is destroying the relationship. There is usually a cycle of periods of separation and subsequent reconciliation, on the basis that it will never happen again, but these promises are inevitably broken, adding to the pain and hopelessness. The temptation to end the marriage frequently surfaces.

The good news is that there is healing and marriage restoration if both partners are willing to seek God and deal with the many issues from their past that are feeding into the present conflict. Sadly, in many cases we find that one of the partners is not prepared to do this. Even in such cases there is still hope and healing for the victim although there may be no realistic expectation for reconciliation of the marriage.

Childhood physical abuse

We have prayed with a number of adults who were victims of physical abuse in their home over an extended period of time. Sometimes it was a mother with deep emotional or mental problems of her own. Or perhaps it was an angry drunken father returning home from the pub. Often the physical abuse was not in isolation and there were episodes of sexual abuse.

Peter was one such man who came for help. He told us afterwards, "God showed me that I had been abused as a child by my father when he used to beat me with a leather strap. I was able to forgive him for this and I was prayed for to release the effects of the abuse. God also showed me how I had been over-zealous in disciplining my own children. I have repented and will ask them to forgive me when I have an opportunity."

In his very moving book *A Boy Called It* (Orion Books, 2002), Dave Pelzer describes the years of abuse he received from his mother. Treated with disdain and hatred he was physically and emotional abused on a daily basis. He was not allowed to eat his meals with the rest of the family. Often, in fact, he was not given food to eat at all.

Treated as a slave, David was expected to do all the household chores and was beaten if they were not completed. No longer regarding David as a human being, his mother referred to him as "it." David's story of survival and over-coming is a wonderful testimony of the power of forgiveness to bring healing even from the depths of horrendous abuse.

A lady told us that her father had beaten her all of her childhood and teenage years. Her skin was often bruised but not in places anyone could see. It usually happened when he was drunk. On more than one occasion he threw her down the stairs.

Many people can recall incidents in their lives when they received harsh and unfair discipline. When we're talking to people who come for help we often ask, "What is your most painful memory of childhood?" Very often the person's reply relates to a time when they were punished unfairly. They recall the emotional pain of the situation rather than the physical pain. The damage on the inside is permanent and is much more significant than the temporary pain of the physical punishment on the outside.

Pat's story

When we asked Pat to share her saddest memory from childhood she responded immediately with the story of an incident that had happened when she was eight years old. She had ridden her bicycle to the local park and was enjoying playing on the swings when some teenage boys arrived. Seeing her bicycle one of the boys decided to have a go on it.

She begged them to give it back but they refused and eventually rode off on it. Pat went home in tears. When her father heard what had happened he was angry with Pat for losing her bicycle, and as a punishment he gave her a spanking and sent her to her room. She had been the victim of the boys' behavior but instead of receiving the love and comfort she needed, she had been physically abused and deeply scarred on the inside.

A young lady we prayed with in the Far East told us how her father created his own idol in their family home. As punishment for the least misdemeanor she would have to stand in front of this idol. If her father caught her not standing she would be beaten on the back of her legs with a stick. She was another individual badly scarred on the inside by the cruelty of a father.

Victim of an unprovoked attack

The physical abuse we receive may be at the hands of a virtual stranger. Our action or behavior may be interpreted by others as aggressive and they react completely inappropriately. It may be that we are simply in the wrong place at the wrong time. We may become the victim of a stranger's road rage or the innocent bystander who gets embroiled in a stranger's frustration and anger.

One young man told us how he was crossing the road one day and a gang of youths attacked him. They knocked him to the ground and kicked him. He almost died. The police didn't believe him when he said he did not know them at all.

Years later he was still suffering as a result of the attack. More painful than the attack itself was the injustice he felt about what had happened. He was angry that the police hadn't believed him. He was also angry that when the case came to court the members of the gang who had attacked him were only given a small fine.

Part of the healing for those who have been abused is to know that they have been heard – to have someone to empathize with them and to understand the injustice of what happened. The ultimate person who does understand is Jesus. It is invaluable to meditate upon the way Jesus suffered abuse as He paid the penalty for our sins at the cross.

Abused in captivity

Those who find themselves in captivity, for whatever reason, become vulnerable to abuse and neglect. They are totally dependent on others who are in authority over them to meet their needs. Irrespective of what they have done or the reason for their captivity, all prisoners have not only physical needs but the need to be treated with some sort of dignity.

Those in authority over prisoners may believe their prisoners don't deserve to be treated with dignity. They may believe for various reasons that they should punish and abuse them. In such a position of authority and power it is all too easy to do this.

During the Second World War many men were captured by the Japanese. Most of them were badly treated. They were despised by their captors as cowards for surrendering rather than fighting to the death. Many of them were subjected to hard physical labor, given very little food and deprived of medical treatment in the prison camps.

Many were brutally beaten and unfairly punished. Sick or

exhausted prisoners would be beaten as a punishment for laziness. Those that survived were little more than walking skeletons. Following the war their bodies were nourished back to health, but what did those men do with the memories and pain? Often they were left with deep emotional scars and were full of bitterness and resentment. "My whole being," said one, "was full of hate for Japan and its people."

We read recently of a Japanese Christian named Keiko. When she attended a conference in Britain for ex-prisoners of war, she realized for the first time the amount of hurt and pain they still carried. "What have we Japanese done?" she asked herself. "These people are in pain and I feel their depression and trauma."

Keiko began to organize trips to Japan for former prisoners and let them hear apologies from friendly caring Japanese. She arranged for them to meet former prison guards and to speak in schools about what had happened to them during the war.

A former prisoner spoke on a television program and gave a very emotional testimony of his experience on one of these trips. "As we walked along, I felt a little hand in mine. I looked down and saw the happy smiling face of this seven-year-old Japanese girl looking up at me. I felt a warmth go through me. I thought, 'I cannot go on with this hatred in my heart. These were not the people who tortured us.' At that moment the hatred seemed to leave me completely."

What causes abusive violence?

Why do people become physically abusive? It may be because they are full of hatred, revenge or jealousy. It may be that they want to see someone else suffer as much as they have suffered. The unresolved anger from their own pain and damage becomes the driving force leading to the abuse of others. Instead of handling anger in a mature way, these people target an innocent and unsuspecting victim. The way they behave and act is often fuelled by demonic spirits of anger, murder and hatred.

A man who came for help explained that he had ended up in prison with a conviction for physical assault. He was at a dance with some friends when someone insulted his girlfriend. His own pain of rejection rushed to the surface and overwhelmed him with anger.

Hardly knowing what he was doing he attacked. He told us that all his life his natural instinct was to punch people on the nose when he felt hurt. The consequence of his action, arising from this uncontrollable anger, was a prison sentence for causing grievous bodily harm to the man he attacked.

Summary

In this chapter we have seen how physical abuse on the outside results in deep damage on the inside. The physical pain is generally only temporary in nature, but the damage to our human spirit and emotional wellbeing can be long lasting. The victims of physical abuse need Jesus to bring healing, not so much to the outside but to the damage on the inside.

In the next chapter we will look at some of the many issues relating to sexual abuse.

Shamefully Used

In John's Gospel we read that Jesus said,

> *"The thief does not come except to steal, and to kill, and to destroy. I have come that they may have life, and that they may have it more abundantly."*

(John 10:10 NKJV)

Nowhere is this strategy of the enemy more evident than in the devastation that occurs as a result of sexual abuse. We have seen so many lives where the thief has come to steal, kill and destroy. The victims who have suffered sexual abuse have indeed been shamefully used with deep and long-lasting consequences.

There will most certainly be people in your church and maybe in your house group who have suffered some form of sexual abuse when they were young. Usually they keep it carefully hidden, never sharing about it and trying to pretend to themselves that it never happened. Although they try to live their life as if they are not affected, in their experience life is far from abundant.

Some time ago we were teaching in a house group about the importance of being willing to forgive all those that have hurt us in any way. In passing we mentioned the categories of people who might need to be forgiven, including those who have abused us in any way.

One lady in the group seemed quite troubled by what we were sharing and asked if she could talk to us in private. She shared that she had been abused by a relative when seven years old but had never been able to tell anyone about it before. We had the privilege of praying about this incident and seeing Jesus bring cleansing and healing into her life.

For those who have experienced sexual abuse there are deep fears, insecurities and a sense of brokenness on the inside that pull them back from developing and growing into strong, mature Christians. Often they are overwhelmed by despair and hopelessness. "Will things always be this way?" they ask themselves. "Can God bring healing into my situation?"

Story of a little wounded bird

During the coffee break on a teaching course at Ellel Grange, I (Liz) was told that a lady was outside crying. As I opened the front door I found a lady sitting on the doorstep crying and also on the step was a pretty little green bird, motionless and silent. I sat on the step and spent some time talking to the lady, trying to comfort her, and then it was time to go in for the next teaching session.

All the time I had been aware of the bird beside me but didn't know what to do about it. It was obviously wounded and perhaps it was dying. Unknown to me, God already had a plan to provide healing for it. Some people had seen a man standing by in the garden who was not on the course. As they rushed past him and went into the house they said, "Please pray for this little bird."

He had approached it with great trepidation because he knew how nervous it felt. He got nearer and nearer until he could stroke its feathers. Having gained its confidence he managed to cup his hands and pick it up. The bird began to struggle to get away and it was then that he saw a bee was hanging from its foot. Eventually, with great difficulty, he managed to extract the bee's sting from the little bird. Then he left it on the grass to recover and, from time to time, checked if it was all right as he sat in his car listening to a cricket game on the radio. Suddenly he looked and rejoiced to find that the bird was not there anymore. It had fully recovered and flown away.

Many people who have been victims of sexual abuse are like that little bird, helpless, confused and unable to fly. They have been wounded and still have something of the enemy attached to them. They need help from someone God can use to set them free from the "sting" of the enemy.

Definition of sexual abuse

Sexual abuse is any activity of a sexual nature imposed upon others without their willing consent. The abuser may be well known to the victim or may be a complete stranger. Whilst adult victims are generally women, men can also be the victims of sexual abuse. Men, however, are less likely to talk about it, or contact the police in the case of rape.

Childhood sexual abuse is activity which exposes children to sexual stimulation inappropriate to their age, psychological development and role in the family. Childhood sexual abuse is a serious sin. God intended that we look after children and that they should remain innocent of sexual matters until they become mature adults. It is something that may happen to small children of both sexes. The abusers are often men but not always. We have heard stories of mothers, sisters, female relatives or female baby sitters who have abused children sexually.

Although the subject of sexual abuse is often mentioned on television, particularly in news broadcasts, some people are still not clear what constitutes sexual abuse. One lady who shared with us felt uncomfortable in the presence of men and wondered if maybe she had been sexually abused as a child by her father and needed prayer about recalling any memories of abuse.

She had no memory of being wrongly touched or any other intimate activities of a sexual nature. She went on to tell us that when she was little her father would sometimes walk around the house naked and sometimes told her dirty stories. She seemed somewhat surprised when we said, "That is abuse," and that it was most likely to be the root cause of her feelings of discomfort around men.

God's plan for sex and sexuality

Before looking in detail at sexual abuse, it is good to remind ourselves of God's plan for sex. After all, sex was His idea in the first place. God's plan is that we should express our sexuality within the security of a loving marriage relationship.

> *For this reason a man will leave his father and mother and be united to his wife, and they will become one flesh.*
>
> (Genesis 2:24)

Through intercourse a married couple becomes one. Every part of their being is joined through the expression of their sexuality. It is not just a physical experience. Yes, there should be physical pleasure, but God's design was even more wonderful than that. He intended an intermingling of their soul and spirit. In sexual intimacy their human spirits are nurtured and built up. There is mutual comfort for both husband and wife. There is a touching of spirits, and a strengthening sense of acceptance belonging and security.

God intended that the expression of our sexuality would bring blessing and great joy.

> *So God created man*
> *in his own image,*
> *in the image of God*
> *he created him;*
> *male and female*
> *he created them.*

> *God blessed them and said to them, "Be fruitful and increase in number . . . "*

> (Genesis 1:27–28)

If we express our sexuality outside the security of a loving marriage relationship we are in rebellion against God's plan for His creation. We are moving out of His safe covering. Instead of receiving blessing from God we open ourselves up to cursing from the enemy in every part of our being. The manufacturer's instruction manual, the Bible, was written for us, His creations. In it God warns us not to get involved in ungodly sexual activity. Scriptures such as Exodus 20:14, Proverbs 5:15–20 and Galatians 5:19 all tell us that willfully entering into sexual activity outside of the marriage covenant is sin which is greatly displeasing to God and will have consequences in our lives.

How much more displeasing to God are activities of a sexual nature that are forced upon an individual against their will. The words of Jesus from Matthew chapter 18 are very relevant:

> *"But if anyone causes one of these little ones who believe in me to sin, it would be better for him to have a large millstone hung around his neck and to be drowned in the depths of the sea. Woe to the world because of the things that cause people to sin! Such things must come, but woe to the man through whom they come!"*

> (Matthew 18:6–7)

What constitutes sexual abuse?

Sexual abuse can take many forms. It is abusive to contact people by telephone and just breathe heavily down the phone rather than speaking to them. Some abusers use the voice of a woman answering the phone as a stimulant to masturbation. When I (Liz) worked for a telephone counseling service overseas, it was clear that some of the callers only rang with this intent in mind. My supervisors said that if I suspected this was happening I was politely but firmly to terminate the call. If the offender was persistent I was to take the phone off the hook for a short while to discourage them. Even the answer-phone message had to be changed from the voice of a woman to that of a man because of this problem.

The way someone looks at others can be abusive. Something is imparted to victims through the eye contact with the abuser. The lustful and unclean thoughts of the heart of the abuser can cause victims to feel that they have been defiled. Women in particular can readily identify with this.

Sexual abuse can be of a verbal nature. It might be comments with a sexual innuendo. It might be the telling of sexual or dirty jokes. It might be relating sexual experiences, sometimes purposely done, within earshot of someone else who has no way of avoiding hearing what has been said. The words can induce images in the mind of the victim leaving them feeling unclean and defiled.

Sexual abuse can involve uninvited physical contact or caressing. In a crowded train or elevator, obtaining some sort of sexual stimulation by brushing up against the body of someone else is abusive.

The physical contact involved with giving someone a hug can be a sexually abusive act if the heart motive is wrong. Even if that motive is pure, a hug can still feel abusive if it is forced upon someone else. Many women can testify to having experienced wrongful hugs even within a church setting.

Abuse can involve the exposing of genitals and masturbating in front of a victim. Many people can recall incidents in their childhood when strangers in a public place suddenly exposed themselves. They experienced trauma and shock and found that unwanted images of defilement entered their mind and became recorded in their memory.

Sexual assault and rape

Both men and women can be victims of sexual assault and rape. Such assaults are recognized in law as serious criminal offences and the victims of such crimes often suffer long-term psychological and spiritual problems. Forced sexual activity may include sexual intercourse, masturbation, oral sex or anal sex. The abuser may be a complete stranger and the experience can be extremely traumatic and frightening. It may include violence or threats of violence to the victim or members of the victim's family. Victims may feel that their life is under threat and that failure to comply with the demands of the abuser will result in murder.

Increasingly these days we hear of so-called "date rape." The victim is not unknown to the abuser. There has been some prior social interaction but sexual activity is entered into without the consent of the victim. It may be against the expressed wishes of the victim and may include violence or threats of violence. For the victim the experience is very traumatic and is compounded by the betrayal of trust which has taken place.

Date rape may involve alcohol or drugs that render victims less capable of resisting the sexual abuser. The victims may have little memory of the abuse but they have still been subject to involvement in some sort of sexual activity without their full consent.

Most incidents of "date rape" go unreported. The conviction rates for reported cases are very low. The onus is generally upon victims to prove that they were unwilling participants in sexual activity. Normally there are no third-party witnesses to what actually happened and very often the victims partly blame themselves.

Sexual abuse within marriage

God's plan for sexual intimacy is that it should take place within the security of a loving marriage relationship and that both partners are consenting to it. Sadly some marriage relationships are abusive and even violent. If one partner forces sexual intercourse upon the other it is abusive. In Britain the law has been changed to include the possibility of rape as a criminal offence within marriage.

Other types of sexual activity within a marriage can be abusive. Examples of this would be forcing one's spouse to watch pornographic movies or to submit to acts of oral and anal sex. We have often been told by women that they have felt defiled by these perversions. We find that there are often demonic manifestations when we pray and minister to people who have had such experiences.

Using sexual favor to manipulate one's spouse is a form of sexual abuse. Within a loving marriage both partners need to be seeking the best for their spouse. Both partners need to be trying to give something into the marriage relationship rather than focusing upon what they can get out of it. When a marriage partner will only agree to sexual activity if the spouse meets certain conditions or behaves in certain ways, then it is a form of sexual abuse.

To withhold sex from a marriage partner is hurtful and rejecting. The Bible tells us not to do it:

> *The husband should fulfil his marital duty to his wife, and likewise the wife to her husband. The wife's body does not belong to her alone but also to her husband. In the same way,*

the husband's body does not belong to him alone but also to his wife. Do not deprive each other except by mutual consent and for a time, so that you might devote yourselves to prayer. Then come together again so that Satan will not tempt you because of your lack of self-control.

(1 Corinthians 7:3–5)

Child sexual abuse

It is always very saddening to hear of the devastating effect that sexual abuse in childhood has had in the lives of many of those who come for help. As both men and women share their experiences, we can only begin to grasp some understanding of the hurt and pain behind all that has happened to them. We are so thankful that we serve a God who fully understands and is willing and able to bring healing into all the damage.

Whilst the abuse can involve a single, very traumatic experience, more often it involves a succession of sexual activities over a period of time. An abuser subjects a child to activities which progressively become more and more intimate.

It may start with touching or caressing the child through clothing. Gradually the child may be led into masturbating the abuser. Eventually the child may be subjected to oral, anal or full sexual intercourse.

The victim feels increasingly uncomfortable with what is happening but the gradual conditioning makes it much more difficult to say "no" and less likely that they will ever disclose to others what is going on.

The abuser will use soft talk to persuade the child or use bribes, threats and intimidation to control. The child is perhaps led to believe that these activities are a "normal" part of life that just isn't talked about. The child may be told that they are going to be treated as an adult or that what is happening between them is their special secret.

There may be threats such as, "I will kill you if you tell anyone what is happening" or "Something terrible will happen to your parents." Fear or false guilt placed upon children effectively silences them and gives continued protection to abusers.

Child abuse may involve just one abuser or it may be more sinister and extreme and involve abuse within a pedophile group or as part of a satanic ritual. Such sexual activity can be very traumatic and physically painful and may be instigated by the group as a form of punishment for some supposed misdemeanor committed by the child.

People who abuse children

The abusers of children usually know their victims. They may be close family members such as parents or grandparents, brothers, sisters, cousins or other relatives. If abusers are not family members they are often respected and trusted individuals who have easy access to their victims. They might be babysitters, teachers, church leaders or youth workers.

They are damaged people motivated by self-gratification and lust. Many abusers of children have themselves been victims of abuse. They struggle in their relationship with adults and find some security in being in complete control through their abuse of children. They live deceptive and secret lifestyles and generally use threats and bribes to keep their victim quiet.

Abusers will deny the seriousness of what they have done. They will try to minimize the consequences of their actions. They will argue that their victim didn't mind, didn't object and even enjoyed it. They might even argue that they were helping their victims discover their sexuality.

Symptoms in victims of childhood sexual abuse

Childhood sexual abuse is traumatic and affects every part of a child's being. It can lead to a breaking of the unity of body, soul and spirit. Children may withdraw internally and dissociate from the emotional pain and memories as a form of escape. As they grow up they may not have any memory of the abuse. However, there are a number of signs or symptoms in adults which indicate that there may have been some form of abuse in the past.

Adults may experience sleep problems and have disturbing dreams. They may be troubled by spirits which give them sexual stimulation as if they were engaged in sexual intercourse. They may be very fearful people who isolate themselves from others and find it very difficult to trust anyone.

Adults may have strange phobias and few memories of their childhood. Usually they will have little self-worth and entertain suicidal thoughts. Some may be emotionally volatile and the buried injustice of what they have experienced may erupt in violent outbursts of apparently inexplicable anger. They may expect to always be victims and often have a history of being victimized in one way or another. To try to cope with the buried pain they may have problems with alcohol or drug dependency.

Victims of child abuse may have buried the pain and memory of the abuse but God knows every single thing that ever happened in their lives and is able to bring healing and restoration. One lady who came for help on a healing retreat was able to write the following:

> *God helped me to face up to the memories of being sexually abused when I was five years old. He didn't just show me that it happened. He also healed me of the fear and the pain and the emptiness it had left me with. Before I came I told God I would like to be myself again, the person I was as a little girl before this happened, and that is what God has done for me.*

Summary

In this chapter we have been looking at the subject of sexual abuse. Those who have suffered such abuse have been shamefully used to gratify the lustful desires of others. Understanding that they have been sinned against is a first step in moving into the healing that Jesus wants to bring into their lives.

In the next chapter we will explore the consequences that abuse of any kind can have on its victims.

Chained to the Past

Although there are many different types of abuse, the damage caused by each has many similarities. This damage can affect every part of a person's being. If you can relate to some or a lot of what we have described in the previous chapters, you may feel weighed down by what has happened to you. You would like to forget it and put it behind you. You would like to get on with your life but struggle to do that. You might not be able to verbalize why this is so, but it's as if you are chained to something and are not free to move forward.

Abuse damages how you see yourself. You have been controlled and dominated by another person, which can leave you feeling you have no free will of your own. You may have developed an expectation that you will always be a victim and end up feeling you have no rights of your own. Sometimes you become passive and need encouragement from others to start standing up for yourself and making godly choices.

It can leave you struggling in the way you relate to others. In abusing you, people have crossed normal relationship boundaries and you are likely to be confused about right boundaries. Your response and behavior towards others may give out a wrong message. You may not recognize when others cross the boundaries of normal behavior and you become prey to further abuse.

You can often develop wrong expectations for your relationships with others. You may assume that it's unsafe to trust anyone. You may find you hold people at a distance and don't allow them to get too close. Abuse is a very painful form of rejection. The rejection exists because people haven't valued you as an individual but have used you to gratify themselves or fulfill their desires. This is tremendously hurtful and you become fearful that it might happen again.

You may have developed fear of rejection. To avoid having to face the pain of rejection you may have often unconsciously employed defense strategies aimed at protecting yourself. Because of your fear of rejection you may now find yourself avoiding close relationships with anyone. What you don't always realize is that the way you may be responding to others and your body language will be sending out a clear message: "Keep your distance."

Distorted belief systems

There was a time in history when people believed the world was flat. Sailors wanted to sail within sight of land because they were fearful that somewhere out to sea they might encounter the edge of the world and fall over it. Can you imagine how a sailor might feel if his captain told the crew that they were going to set out to sea and keep sailing away from land and into the unknown?

The thought of sailing over some huge waterfall would generate all sorts of anxiety and fear. His wrong belief system would affect his emotional reactions. Out of his fear he might organize a mutiny, take over the ship and set sail for home and safety. His wrong belief system about the danger he was in, would affect his actions.

When you have been abused, your belief system becomes distorted. Your experiences mold your thinking and you may try to rationalize what has happened to you. You develop untrue beliefs about God, about yourself and about others. These belief systems, often operating at the unconscious level, affect your emotions and your actions.

You often develop wrong beliefs about God. Your concept of what God is like is greatly influenced by the way authority figures in your life treat you. If your parents or church leaders give you a wrong role model of God through some form of abuse, you will have a distorted concept of God.

You make assumptions that God will behave in the same way that these authority figures did in your life. You may decide that God doesn't care about you and doesn't really love you. You might think that the abuse you suffered is some sort of punishment from God. You might conclude that God is untrustworthy. You daren't allow yourself to get too close to God for fear that He, too, might betray you and hurt you.

You may start to believe the lie that somehow you were the reason the abuse took place. If you had been different, perhaps it wouldn't have happened. You might decide that you are "bad" or "dirty" or "rebellious." You might believe the lie that you deserve to be punished for what happened. It is very easy to believe the lies that the verbal abuser has spoken into your life that you are "useless" or "a waste of space."

Often you have distorted views of others. You may have decided that "I can't trust a man," or "I can't trust a woman," or "I can't trust anyone in authority." Such beliefs come out of the judgments we have made because of the pain of the abuse. These "black or white" and "all or nothing" statements are a distortion of truth. It is true that you can't trust *some* people but it is actually a lie to say that you can't trust *anyone*.

In 2 Corinthians 10:5 we are instructed to "take captive every thought to make it obedient to Christ." This means, we believe, that we need to test whether our thoughts are fully in agreement with what Jesus would say. If they are not, we need to recognize this fact. We need to review and reject the thoughts and replace them with thoughts that Jesus would agree with.

Denial

When you've experienced abuse you might try to deal with it by denial. It can be really painful to face the truth of what happened to you. So you might choose to deny that you were badly damaged by what happened. You might try to tell yourself that you can easily get over it or that there is no point in dwelling on the past so you'll just get on with life.

Whilst it is true that you don't want to spend the rest of your life focusing on things from the past, there is a need to deal with past issues when they are like chains, holding you back from moving into God's good plans and purposes for your future. You need to face the past issues, no matter how painful they may be, and allow God to bring His healing into them.

Because of the pain involved you can dissociate and distance yourself from what happened. You attempt to put everything in a room in your life and then try to shut the door upon it. You may choose not to remember or you may choose to bury the pain associated with these memories.

Sometimes people have the memory of what happened but no pain associated with that memory. In ministry people have told us of dreadful stories of physical or sexual abuse in a matter-of-fact way with no expression of emotions. There has been a disconnection between what has happened and the emotional hurt and pain involved.

Sometimes in ministry people will tell us that they have buried pain and grief inside them but don't know what caused it. There may be no sense of joy in their lives. They might say that somehow inside they have a sense of loss. Sometimes buried or denied childhood memories are triggered by current events. It is in hearing about another person's trauma that they suddenly have an emotional response as if it was happening to them.

Distorted emotional responses

Our emotions are the inner feelings or reactions that we have to our perception of what is happening around us. Sometimes these emotional reactions can be distorted. The emotions we feel in the present and the depth of that emotional reaction are affected by the things that have happened to us in the past. Because of this, our reactions can be out of proportion to the event happening today. Some of the feelings belong to the past.

It is important to realize that your perception of what is happening may not be accurate. You might, for example, assume that your boss is angry with you because he had a frown on his face when you spoke to him this morning. The reality may be that his mind was completely absorbed with another issue that was troubling him. Yet because of your painful memories of rejection, you can quickly assume the worst of him. You might assume that the pastor at church rejected you last Sunday when he rushed past without acknowledging you. The reality is that he was so deep in thought about the sermon that he was about to preach that he didn't even notice you.

As a consequence of abuse you can be very fearful of further abuse. If you perceive that a current situation might develop into an abusive situation you can become very anxious. That is partly why abuse victims can develop many fears and phobias.

You might have an extreme fear of men if you have been sexually abused by a man. If someone in authority has mistreated you, you may develop a fear of all authority figures. Subconsciously you see all men or all authority figures as a danger. You may perceive the loving caring person who only wants to help you as a threat and wrongly assume that he is seeking for someone to control and dominate.

If you have been physically assaulted by a stranger in the past you may develop a deep fear of going out at night.

Sometimes people have a deep fear in even telling others what has happened to them – especially if they were threatened with what might happen if they told anyone.

Suppressed anger

When there has been abuse there is invariably a measure of suppressed anger. It is not always recognized as such but, nevertheless, it is still there. People know in their spirit that something is not right.

The anger they have may be about what someone else has done to them. We believe that God is angry about the abuse people suffer and that it is right for them to feel angry also. This is righteous anger. Often, as we minister, we find there is a need to explain this and to give a person permission to be angry about what happened and encourage them to feel this anger.

The anger they feel may be more towards those who should have protected them from the abuse. Victims of child sexual abuse may feel angry that their mothers didn't protect them from their stepfather. Many victims tell us that their mothers knew or suspected what was going on but chose to ignore it.

The man abused in prison by fellow inmates may feel angry with the prison authorities who failed to protect him. The victim of spiritual manipulation and abuse may feel angry with the elders of the church for not confronting the issue.

The anger some feel may be directed at God. They may blame Him for not protecting them or for allowing the abuse to continue. They may blame God for not healing them of the consequences of the abuse.

Anger may be directed towards themselves. They may feel angry that they did nothing to stop the abuse. They may feel angry with themselves for "being stupid" and not realizing that they were being abused.

Self-harm and suicidal thoughts

Anger with self is sometimes expressed in self-harm and suicidal thoughts. Although people are victims of abuse, they may blame themselves and feel guilty for allowing it to continue and not stopping it. They feel angry towards themselves and feel they deserve to be punished. The self-harm becomes a form of punishment. They judge and condemn themselves, becoming executioners of the sentence they have passed upon themselves.

For others, self-harm is a coping mechanism to try and deal with hurt and pain which is locked on the inside. The physical pain from self-harming takes the focus off the deep inner pain. The physical pain is more bearable than the emotional pain and covers it up.

Victims of abuse invariably have feelings of low self-esteem. They have been rejected and so they reject themselves, often developing a great self-hatred. They don't like themselves and even entertain thoughts like, "I might as well be dead."

Many victims of severe abuse have either attempted to take their own life on more than one occasion or have seriously thought about suicide. For some it is a cry for help, but for others death is a preferable option to living with their ever-present hurt and pain on the inside.

Guilt and shame

Victims of abuse frequently struggle with feelings of shame and what we call false guilt. False guilt is an emotion which says, "I was responsible for what happened – I have done something wrong." It says, "I must have done something to cause the abuse and I should have done something to stop it."

Shame is the humiliating feeling of having appeared un-favorable in my own eyes or the eyes of others. It comes about when my mistake, failure or wrongdoing is publicly exposed.

Shame stops me from feeling good about myself. Shame tells me that I'm dirty and unlovable. Shame tells me that I am unacceptable to others and unacceptable to God. Shame tells me that I am a failure and that I am bad.

Victims of abuse have often been falsely accused of being responsible for what has happened and they carry both shame and false guilt. Carol, for example, came forward for a brief time of prayer on a ministry night at one of the Ellel conferences. She had just heard some teaching on sexual abuse and wanted to share her story.

Her early childhood had been dominated by her father's addiction to alcohol. He would often get drunk and violent. Carol and her mother were terrified of him. When Carol was eleven she was sexually abused by two men.

She eventually got married but the marriage didn't last. Her husband turned out to be a very violent and abusive man, and he became bitter towards God and left her because she was a Christian. She began to cry as she explained that her husband's family were blaming her for the break-up of the marriage. It seems that all her life she had been blamed. As we ministered to Carol we had to keep reminding her that she was not guilty in God's eyes. A key part of the ministry was for Carol to hear that and to begin to believe it.

Inner vows

As a consequence of abuse you may find you have made inner vows, such as "I will never trust a man again," or "I will never trust a church leader again," or even "I will never be healed." Out of your hurt and pain you say things like, "I will never show my pain. I will never give them the satisfaction of knowing how much they really hurt me on the inside." Such words have power and by making such self-pronouncements you are choosing to bury and suppress your emotions. Although you move on in life, seeming to forget all about it, you keep to this vow and you are chained and restricted to it like a prisoner with a ball and chain.

For all of us the act of continually pushing down our emotional pain and hurt doesn't make it disappear by any means. Often it just manifests in different ways. It may surface as migraines, back pain or some other physical sickness. It may surface in violent outbreaks of anger or even depression and mental breakdown.

Individuals who experience a major breakdown in their lives will often attribute it to some recent incident. But usually the recent incident was just the straw that broke the camel's back. They often don't realize that the last incident just added to all the hurt and pain that had been previously pushed down. They had run out of energy to hold things down anymore so, like an erupting volcano, everything came to the surface and the person went into overload.

Ungodly defenses

After experiencing abuse of any kind, most of us will try to avoid the pain of further abuse by withdrawing and isolating ourselves from others. We keep away from others as a form of defense so they can't abuse us. We may stop going to church because the kind of abuse we suffered was spiritual and we are afraid it will happen again. For example, if it was a church leader who tried to dominate and control us, we may find that every time we see that person, it just triggers into the pain and hurt within us. We may then decide to stay away from church and avoid going into situations where we could possibly meet that person in the future. Then it may extend to not going to any church.

Some women, who were sexually abused in childhood, may choose to dress in a way which is intended to avoid any unwelcome attention. For instance, they may choose to wear baggy clothes and purposefully neglect their appearance.

Subconsciously they might also try to make themselves physically unattractive to men by over-eating. Such behavior, fuelled by their low self-esteem, is an unconscious attempt to try and protect themselves from further abuse.

To try to deal with the hurt from past abuse we may revert to using coping mechanisms. We deliberately engage in activities that bring pleasure or comfort in an effort to mask the pain. Some of these coping mechanisms are ungodly because they lead us into seeking comfort in things which God never intended. Perhaps it is chemical substances such as nicotine, alcohol or drugs, which we use to dull emotional pain as a kind of anesthetic.

We may try to get some small pleasure in life through pornography and masturbation but then find we are trapped into an addictive behavior pattern which is sinful. Despite wishing to give up these habits, we find ourselves unable to do that and we are driven by a compulsion to have them in our life. Fearing the disapproval of others we may keep our addictions secret, but this just adds to the guilt we already carry. The enemy is very quick to heap further condemnation upon us.

Some of us may develop a different kind of defense to keep ourselves from further abuse. This may have its roots in the past when someone in authority has taken advantage of us and treated us badly. We may become rebellious in our heart. We make a decision not to submit to others and determine to be independent and self-sufficient. This refusal to come under any authority often extends to the godly authorities we should be willing to come under, and as a result we can become unteachable and open to self-deception.

Distorted identity

Abuse violates every part of us as human beings and leaves us confused about our true identity. It results in deep and severe damage to our human spirit in the core part of our being. God has created each one of us for relationships which bring blessing and so abusive ones wound us very deeply. The abusive words of rejection spoken to us, and the actions done against us, are like dagger wounds penetrating into our spirit. As a result we find it a struggle to be able to believe the truths in God's Word.

The Bible tells us that we are precious and wonderfully made (Psalm 139:14) but we may feel anything but that. We may feel dirty and defiled. We may hate everything about ourselves and so we feel confused about the truth revealed in the Bible which seems to contradict our experiences in life.

If we have been spiritually abused, we may have a distorted concept of God, which causes us to struggle to grasp that we have an identity in Christ. Questions may form in our minds such as, "Does God love me unconditionally, or does He only love me when I obey?"

If we have been sexually abused we may feel confused about our sexuality and the expression of it. We may have been forced into expressions of our sexuality in an unloving and ungodly environment. As a result we may reject our own sexuality. Girls have often said to themselves, "I don't want to be a woman if this is what it means." Boys have felt ashamed of their masculinity. This was the case for Simon who gave permission for his story to be shared in the book *Martial Arts and Yoga* by our friend Brenda Skyrme (Sovereign World, 2000).

> Simon was born into a home where neither parent wanted him. He faced rejection from his conception to the time he was born and rejection by both his parents and his two sisters, from his birth until the time he left home. He was abused mentally, sexually and physically by his father, whose verbal abuse included continual negative pronouncements that caused Simon to withdraw socially. The attitude of his father encouraged his two older sisters

to treat him as an object to be laughed at and criticised at the least opportunity.

Therefore, it became a pattern in Simon's life that he considered himself not to be worthy of any love or kindness; he only knew that he was called a bad boy and was considered to be unacceptable. Because of the sexual abuse he received, he was also ashamed of his own sexuality and masculinity.

Our experience is that the consequences of sexual confusion can be expressed in a number of ways. Some get married but the marriage relationship can be spoiled by frigidity and fear of intimacy within marriage. Others respond by developing a fear of the opposite sex which leads them to become involved in lesbianism or male homosexuality. Others react by becoming promiscuous in seeking to find love and acceptance in relationships. Some even become prostitutes because they reason that, "If people are going to use my body for their self-gratification, then I might as well get paid for it."

Physical damage

Physical damage and illness can be a direct consequence of abuse. In the case of sexual abuse there may be anal or vaginal damage. This kind of damage may cause problems with infertility or the digestive tract. There may also be damage as a result of sexually transmitted diseases.

When there has been physical abuse there can be scarring or some form of physical disability. The victims have to live with a constant physical reminder of what happened to them. There may be problems with tinnitus (ringing in the ear), frequent headaches and migraines or partial deafness as a result of blows sustained to the head.

There can be physical damage as an outworking of the inner damage. We have already seen how those who have been abused may use tobacco, alcohol or drugs as coping mechanisms to deal with the pain. Such comforts may bring temporary relief or escape but there is usually a cost in terms of resulting physical sickness and ill health.

Self-harming or suicide attempts can have an outworking in terms of physical damage. Overdosing with drugs, for example, may have affected internal organs such as the liver. One person we prayed with had thrown herself off a balcony and as a result suffered with major back problems.

Creation of ungodly soul-ties

Abuse can result in the creation of ungodly soul-ties.[1] What does that mean? Well, God's plan is that we should bless one another in all our relationships. As we relate to others a bonding takes place – we give something of ourselves to the other person and become open to receive something from that person. As a relationship becomes closer and more intimate the bonding becomes stronger. We refer to this relationship bond as a "soul-tie." It is a tie that involves the non-physical part of our being. It involves our mind, will, emotions and human spirit.

The concept of "soul-ties" is found in the Bible although the actual words are not used. Often the word "joined" is used, as in Matthew 19:6 – "what God has joined together" – and 1 Corinthians 1:10 – "be perfectly joined" (NKJV).

Another expression the Scripture uses is being "yoked together" with others and we are instructed to take Jesus' yoke upon us (Matthew 11:28–29). We can also be "knit together" in our heart (Colossians 2:2 NKJV) or "like-minded" (Philippians 2:2).

God's intention is that these relationship bonds or soul-ties should be godly and a source of blessing. However, when

1. For more on soul-ties see the book in this series entitled *Soul-Ties* by David Cross.

relationships go wrong, and are outside God's plans, we create ungodly bonds or ties. These types of ungodly ties are a channel of cursing rather than blessing. We are not to be unequally yoked (2 Corinthians 6:14) or to be "entangled" with others (Galatians 5:1 NKJV). Isaiah 10:27 speaks of the "yoke" of slavery.

Ungodly ties are formed in any relationship where people agree to rebel against God's law. By moving outside God's protection, they expose themselves to the work of the enemy in their lives. Ungodly ties are also established when one of the individuals in a relationship sins against the other. Although the innocent party has done nothing wrong, he or she becomes susceptible to cursing as a consequence of the other person's sin.

Very strong ungodly soul-ties are established wherever there has been abuse. Abusers override the free will of their victims, violating and defiling spirit and soul. Years after the abuse has taken place, victims may still even sense the presence of the one who abused them.

These ties can be pictured as ungodly chains binding people together. It's as if the other person is still there. It's as if there has been a joining and a mingling on the inside. Hurtful words and wrong actions can be like an unending tape recording playing in their minds and holding them in captivity to the events of the past.

In order to move into God's plans and purposes for our life it is important that these kinds of ungodly ties should be broken. We will look at how to do this in a later chapter.

Demonization

When we pray and minister to those who have been abused we often find that there is a need for deliverance, especially when the abuse has been severe. Abuse against someone else is sin and it's rebellion against God's plan. Because of this, demonic rights become established in the life of the innocent victim of the abuse and deliverance is a necessary part of the healing process.

For some of our readers demonization and the need for deliverance may be a new concept. However, it is abundantly clear to us as we read the New Testament that deliverance played an important part in the healing ministry of Jesus. He recognized that many were in captivity to the work of the enemy in their lives and needed to be set free. In Acts 10:38 the apostle Peter summarized Jesus' ministry in these words:

> *He went around doing good and healing all who were under the power of the devil, because God was with him.*

The Bible tells us that we are in a spiritual battle with the kingdom of darkness which is ruled by Satan who exercises power through the demonic realm (Ephesians 6:12). The demons who serve the kingdom of darkness desire to express their nature through a human being. You will see this if you read one of the gospels and look to see how often Jesus cast demons out of people. If the person is in rebellion to God and in sin, they unfortunately create within them a place of spiritual darkness. In other words they give the enemy a place of authority in their lives.

In Ephesians 4:26–27 the Bible says, " 'In your anger do not sin.' ... Do not give the devil a foothold." In this verse the Greek word *topos* is translated as "foothold" which means a physical place. When the enemy has been given a place, demons are able to exercise something of their nature in those areas of the person's life where they have been given rights or authority. This is what the Bible means when it describes people as being demonized.

Victims of abuse often do not realize that they need deliverance. Sometimes they will say that the abuse took place before they became Christians. "Surely I belong to Jesus now, so how can I be demon possessed?"

They are right in saying that they belong to Jesus as Christians. In the English language possession means ownership and we would certainly agree that Christians belong to Jesus.

Confusion and misunderstanding arise because the word "demon possessed" is a poor translation of the original Greek word *daimonizomai* which means "to have a demon" or "be demonized." We would not use the expression "demon possessed" but prefer to say "have a demon." We can be saved or born again and still have a demon if the enemy has not been evicted or if he still has rights in our life. An illustration of this is when we buy a house. The house changes ownership on completion of the sale but there may still be repairs to be made or areas of dry rot, woodworm or termites that need to be dealt with. Just because we own the house, it doesn't mean that all unpleasant pests vanish overnight. We have to take action against them and throw them out.

Demonization is one of the consequences of abuse but the good news is that God has made provision for healing and deliverance. Through His death on the cross Jesus has triumphed over the enemy. The Bible tells us that Jesus has made a spectacle of him (Colossians 2:15).

During His earthly ministry Jesus set people free by ministering deliverance to them. In the Great Commission Jesus gave authority and power to the disciples and the Church to continue this ministry of setting the captives free. We often come across people who have had counseling and prayer about the abuse in their life but have never received deliverance ministry. They may have received some healing but in order to be truly free and able to move on in their Christian lives, we have found that they also require a measure of deliverance.

Expectations of always being a victim

The victims of abuse often develop an expectation that they will always have to be a victim. When the abuse is ongoing they can't generally see any way out of their predicament. As we talk and pray with them we try to help them clarify their options and encourage them to be active and not passive.

We encourage them to set boundaries of what is acceptable behavior and to have an action plan if someone crosses those boundaries. Victims of domestic violence may need to involve their pastor, the police or social services and consider moving out to a safe haven. In the workplace victims of verbal abuse may need to confront the abuser or be encouraged to approach their Union representative or Human Resources Department. Those struggling with spiritual abuse may have to face the reality of their situation and either confront the abuser or choose to withdraw from the place where the abuse goes on.

Each situation is different and there may be many factors to consider. We see our role as helping people to be aware of the choices open to them but not making the choices for them. It is important that they understand that God does not want them to continue as a victim of abuse and that He will strengthen them and help them as they take difficult decisions.

Summary

In this chapter we have been looking at some of the major consequences of having been the victim of some form of abuse. We can be affected in every part of our being. Our thoughts, behavior, decisions and emotional responses will all carry consequences of the abuse. There may well be physical sickness as a direct or indirect result of the abuse. There will almost always be a need for some deliverance.

In the next chapter we will look at the importance of knowing for ourselves the love and compassion of our heavenly Father as we seek healing for the abuse we have experienced.

The Father Who Cares

As we minister to people whose lives have been devastated by abuse we usually find that they have developed a wrong concept of God. Their thinking about God is very confused. They say things like: "I trusted someone in authority and look what happened! How can I ever trust anyone again, including God?"

They may rationalize to themselves thinking: "God is all powerful – He could have done something. Perhaps He didn't act because He was trying to teach me something or perhaps He was punishing me for something."

Such thinking creates a false picture of God. God can and does use the circumstances of life to teach us, but we believe it is wrong to say that God creates all the circumstances and experiences we face in life in order to teach us.

If we have a faulty concept of what God is like we need to turn back to God's Word and base our understanding of God upon His revelation of Himself. The very essence of God's nature is summed up in the Hebrew word *hesed* – a word that means "everlasting love and kindness." God doesn't choose to be loving and kind *sometimes*. He is always loving and kind, because it is His essential nature and character and He can't ever be otherwise. He is perfect love but also perfect justice.

Whenever God acts it is always righteous and absolutely fair. One day He will judge all sin and evil, but until that day He desires to show mercy and forgiveness to all those who desire to repent. He is gracious and compassionate, slow to anger and rich in love. He wants to have a close relationship with each one of us. He is faithful to fulfill His covenantal promises to His people and wants to bless them.

God's nature revealed in Jesus

God reveals His true nature in Jesus. Jesus, the perfect sinless man, came to reveal the true nature of God to all of us, His creation. When Philip said to Jesus, "show us the Father and that will be enough for us," the reply he received from Jesus was, "Anyone who has seen me has seen the Father" (John 14:8, 9).

If you struggle with understanding the true nature of God, look to Jesus. Look at how He treated the woman caught in adultery with compassion (John 8:1–11). Look at how He rebuked the disciples for not allowing the people to bring their children to Him for a blessing (Matthew 19:13–14). Look at the way He was moved to pity by the suffering of the people of Israel (Luke 13:34).

Jesus came to reveal what the Father is truly like. He did it through the way He treated people and He did it through His stories and parables. The father in the wonderful story of the prodigal son is a picture of our loving heavenly Father (Luke 15:11–32). As Jesus told this story, the listeners would have expected the father to react in anger towards his rebellious son. They would have expected him to scold his son and punish him for wasting the money. Instead, the picture that Jesus paints of the father would have come as quite a shock because he was very different. This father treats the wayward son with kindness and compassion. He reaches out to him in love before the boy can say a word. He throws his arms around him and is overjoyed to welcome him home. This is a picture of the way our heavenly Father treats a repentant sinner with kindness, love and mercy.

Imagine now, if you can, how much love and compassion our heavenly Father will show those who have suffered because they have been treated cruelly and abused by others!

The compassionate Father

The words found in Isaiah 40:11 have become for us a true expression of the concept of our heavenly Father and what He is really like:

> *He tends his flock like a shepherd:*
> *He gathers the lambs in his arms*
> *and carries them close to his heart;*
> *he gently leads those that have young.*

This is a beautiful picture of God, the compassionate, caring Father, bringing comfort to the hurting who are crushed, down-trodden and broken-hearted.

Those of us who are fathers may have experienced the strong desire to comfort our children when they were suffering and helpless. I (Paul) remember one night when our own daughter Angela was a baby.

We were living in Yokohama, Japan, at that time and were woken up late at night by a wheezing noise coming from Angela's bedroom. She was suffering an attack of croup and was barely able to breathe.

We quickly jumped in the car and took her to the Emergency Unit at the local hospital. The young doctor on duty was casually sitting reading the newspaper with his feet on his desk as we entered the hospital. One look at Angela and he sprang into action and, with a serious expression on his face, rushed her away to be X-rayed.

Within minutes Angela was installed in an oxygen tent and the young doctor was preparing equipment ready to carry out an emergency tracheotomy (the insertion of a tube into her windpipe to enable her to breathe more easily). The consultant pediatrician had been called and was on his way. Thankfully, within the humid atmosphere of the oxygen tent Angela's breathing began to improve and an operation was not necessary. She was treated and discharged from hospital the next day, none the worse for her ordeal.

As I think back on this experience, I remember the absolute helplessness I felt when I saw the distress that my daughter was in. She was distraught and upset and there was nothing I could do about it. As a father I would have done anything to relieve the pain and discomfort that Angela was suffering. In my love and concern for her I would have gladly changed places with her.

Years later I have pondered on my emotions that night and compared them to the emotions of our heavenly Father who is perfect love.

The Father's love for you

I wonder how our loving heavenly Father felt when Jesus was enduring the cross and all that it entailed. Did He want to intervene and stop it when Jesus was being unjustly accused and when He was being mocked and whipped by the soldiers? What was happening in the heart of God when Jesus was being stripped and cruelly nailed to the cross? How did the Father feel as Jesus hung on the cross? He knew that Jesus went through excruciating pain each time He was forced to pull himself up by those nail-pierced hands in order to take a gasp of breath.

When my daughter couldn't breathe I would have done anything to alleviate her pain. I wonder if Father God was tempted to abandon the plan of salvation as He watched His only begotten Son gasping for breath on the cross. If I were

God I think I would have wanted to shout, "Enough – they're not worth saving. Bring My Son home and annihilate them all." Unlike me, who was helpless at the plight of my daughter, God had the authority and power to do something about the situation and the plight of Jesus, but He chose not to act. His love for you made Him go on resisting His longing to help His Son.

It wasn't that He didn't love Jesus or thought somehow that He deserved to be punished. It wasn't that Jesus was trying to appease an angry Father and somehow twist His arm and make Him accept back all of us human beings who had rebelled against Him and turned our backs on Him. No – our loving heavenly Father knew that victory through the cross was the only way of salvation. The redemption price had to be paid.

God so loved you and me that He was willing to allow this redemption price to be paid. Child of God, have you fully grasped the love that God has for you that was expressed at the cross?

The lies of the enemy

It was the greatest act of love in the history of the universe, and yet we can so easily lose sight of it. When we feel that God hasn't done what we would like Him to do, we can even forget this tremendous act of love. We may become bitter and resentful towards God and feel that He has let us down. We may think that He doesn't care when we experience hurt and pain.

These thoughts are not truth but lies of the enemy. Jesus described Satan as the "father of lies" (John 8:44). One of the names given to Satan is "accuser." Satan loves to bring guilt and condemnation into our lives through false accusation. He also likes to sow doubt and confusion into our minds by bringing false accusation against God: "God doesn't really care about you" or "If God really loved you He would have . . ."

We need to take such thoughts captive and make them obedient to the truth about God. No matter what we are experiencing or going through, we need to try and remember what happened at the cross. Somehow we need to hold fast to the knowledge of God's love for us, expressed at Calvary, even when we don't understand His apparent or perceived indifference to circumstances in our life.

When we have prayed with people who have been abused, they have often asked us, "Why did God allow this?" or "Why didn't God stop this happening?" Sometimes the questions aren't even put into words but abused people form a conclusion which becomes part of their concept of God. They decide that God isn't really powerful, that He isn't really trustworthy, or that He doesn't really care about them.

It's important to bring all such secret thoughts about God into the open where they can be tested and examined. We can all hold certain beliefs to be true only to find out that, when we receive further information, they are false.

We have shared our own conclusions about God with those we have been getting to know, so that they can perhaps see a new perspective. We have said that we believe God is sovereign and has the authority and power to do whatever He wants to do, but that He chooses to limit Himself and the way in which He acts.

We are utterly convinced that the reason He does so is that when He created human beings, He decided to give them the gift of free will. What an enormous risk that was! Each person in the world is free to accept or reject the truth of God, to be obedient to His commands or to rebel against them, to love one another or to abuse one another sinfully. God cannot stop people from sinning or there would not be such a thing as a free-will choice.

If we are honest with ourselves, we can all recognize that there are times when we have made mistakes or deliberately chosen to sin against someone, but God has not stepped in and stopped us. Although our sin hurt, offended and caused damage to another person, God did not immediately act. In our sin we also hurt God Himself who loves the person that we sinned against.

It is the same for us as parents. We suffer when anyone sins against our children. If they are hurt or offended by someone, then we, too, feel hurt and offended. We have no doubt at all that this must be how God feels about His children.

Do you think of this when you ask God to forgive your sins? When asking God to forgive the pain, hurt and damage that you have caused others through your sin, you need to acknowledge that you have also caused hurt, pain and offence to God.

We can't claim to understand and see everything from God's perspective and so we certainly don't want to give a glib answer to anyone who has endured abuse. However, we know that it was not God's plan that anyone should suffer abuse. We can never agree that the abuse was a punishment from our loving heavenly Father. We believe that when a small helpless child is being abused, our heavenly Father is furious. This horrible sin causes Him great grief and pain.

Where were You, God?

We remember very vividly ministering to Steve, who had been badly bullied at school. Over and over again he would ask the question, "Where was God when I was being bullied? Why didn't He do something about it?" We suggested he asked God to show him. We paused for a few moments and then he said, "God has just given me a picture. I was being punched in the face by this bully but Jesus was standing between me and the bully. Each time I was punched Jesus was also being punched."

This picture helped Steve realize that God identified with his hurt and pain. It brought home to him the truth that the things that hurt him also hurt God. This picture of Jesus being punched gave Steve new understanding of the verse about Jesus which says:

> *He was despised and rejected by men,*
> *a man of sorrows, and familiar with suffering.*
>
> (Isaiah 53:3)

When someone has been abused it is a big step of faith to trust again. For many it can be a big step of faith even to trust God. One lady we ministered to said: "I can see Jesus with His arms open wide to embrace me but I'm not sure that I can fully trust Him yet. Please pray that I will get to that place of being able to trust Him." Our prayer for all of you who have been abused is that you will be able to get to that place.

God understands how you feel. He knows the difficulties you struggle with. He knows that it is only natural to try to protect yourself from further pain. He also knows that, unless you can get to that place of trusting and surrendering to Him, you will never be totally free. As you struggle to trust God, be encouraged by the words of Isaiah 42:3:

> *A bruised reed he will not break,*
> *and a smouldering wick he will not snuff out.*
> *In faithfulness he will bring forth justice . . .*

You might like to pray this prayer:

Father God, help me to put my trust in You and to be open to all that You want to do in my life. You understand the struggles I have. Help me to have a right understanding and concept of You as my loving and caring heavenly Father who wants the best for me. Thank You for the love You have for me, expressed in all that happened at the cross. Help me to get to that place where I can receive that love into my own life. Amen.

Summary

In this chapter we have been looking at the importance of having a right concept of our loving heavenly Father. You have a heavenly Father who is filled with love, compassion and kindness for you. It was not His plan for you to be the victim of abuse. He can identify with your pain and hurt, and wants to bring His comfort and healing into your life.

In the next chapter we will look at how we can begin to release the emotional pain of abuse and begin to move from being a victim, chained to the abuse of the past, to becoming an overcomer, moving forward into our destiny in Jesus.

Releasing the Emotional Pain

9

We can have many different emotional reactions to being abused. These include rejection, confusion of identity, shame and false guilt. Added to these issues will be various fears and phobias and almost certainly anger, whether we recognize it or not. The anger about the abuse usually sits over all the other feelings and is actually fuelled by them.

People who have been abused are often very confused by the mixture of the feelings they have. The relationship with the abuser may at times have been one of love and respect, but the abusive aspects of the relationship have introduced a very different element. For example, young children yearn for love and affirmation from the very parents who are abusing them and so they feel both love and hatred at the same time.

Battered wives may love their husbands because there is kindness and love shown in the relationship at times. But at other times, there is cruelty and violence, sometimes as a result of their husbands' consumption of too much alcohol, and any trust and respect in the relationship is damaged beyond repair. So we can end up with very mixed and confused feelings.

Acknowledging the hurt and pain

When there has been abuse an important part of the healing process is the release of emotions. The victim needs to be honest about the pain and hurt that they have experienced. Maybe they have denied that they were hurt because they don't want to face the pain. Perhaps they were not allowed to express their true feelings at the time of the abuse, or they learnt to push down the hurt and internalize it.

If this applies to you, we would encourage you not to suppress your feelings but to be willing to release the hurt and pain, possibly through the shedding of tears. We are not saying that you must relive your painful experiences but simply that you need to deal with any suppressed emotions.

Verbalizing your thoughts and feelings with an understanding listener is often the starting point to healing. It helps you to clarify your own emotions and reactions and make some sort of sense of what you have experienced. It is particularly helpful to do this if expression of emotions wasn't allowed in childhood. If you have been sinned against and not allowed to express your feelings, there can be a desire inside to be heard, especially if you tried to tell someone what was happening to you and you were punished or not believed.

Jean's story is a good illustration. She wrote the following:

> It was a revelation to me to see that I was an angry person on the inside. For all these years I had kept it down and well hidden. But with the Lord's permission I have started to let go of it. What a release! I felt for the first time I was really being listened to. The counselors really heard me and they didn't try to rush me, in fact they said to take my time and encouraged me to talk. I thank God for them and their compassion.

As listeners we need to be empathetic to what is being said. We need to reflect back to people what they have been saying in various ways such as, "So you felt angry when your mother...?" Such feedback helps to clarify the different emotions they may have been experiencing.

If the feelings being talked about or expressed are those of rightful anger (anger which is appropriate in the circumstances), we need to reassure people that it is acceptable for them to have that feeling. We might say, "Yes, you had every right to feel angry about what was done to you. It was sinful and God was angry about it too."

Very often there is confusion and guilt about having feelings of anger. It is part of the healing for people to hear someone else confirm that it is all right to have the emotion of anger and that it is not a sin.

Expression of feelings

Some people find it helpful to express their feelings by writing them down. We have often encouraged people to write a letter to God telling Him how they felt. This can be helpful when you have deeply buried feelings of anger towards God.

It is a good idea to write down the questions that have been nagging away internally and serving as a blockage to healing. We may have such questions as, "Where were You in all this, God?" or "Why didn't You do something to stop it?" It may be that you are verbalizing these for the first time, and acknowledging the questions can bring a measure of healing in itself.

Some people can express their pain and anger through a creative activity such as painting. They cannot find words, but in expressing themselves with paint, they get in touch with their inner feelings. This can be very helpful when you are experiencing a number of emotions simultaneously.

Karen, for example, painted a picture of her childhood with a thick stripe of grey paint on which she wrote the words "sullen, unwell, silly, inadequate and inferior." She then covered this grey stripe with blobs of red paint. The red paint symbolized anger. It was an expression of her being able to stamp her feet over the experiences of those years, and to be angry at all the things that had happened to her.

When we feel angry our whole body tenses up. Our pulse quickens and our blood pressure rises. Some kind of physical activity helps release this tension in the body and the accompanying anger. Many people have expressed their anger in wrong ways by throwing things and causing damage which they regret afterwards. There are ways we can physically release anger without hurting ourselves or others, and without the destruction of property.

Physical release of anger

At Ellel Grange we have a big log pile where we keep wood to burn on our open fires during the winter months. Some people find release for their suppressed anger by picking up these logs and throwing them. Chopping up the logs is another way in which people can find a physical release for their anger.

Some have shared with us that they have released their buried anger by skimming stones across the surface of a pond or lake or throwing pebbles into the sea. One of our ministry team bought some foam building bricks for her grandson. She discovered that she could safely throw these and release physical energy and anger without causing any damage.

Another safe way of dissipating tension and anger without causing damage is to take a damp tea towel and whack the doorpost with it. There are other ways in which you can physically release anger, such as playing squash, going for a walk, kneading bread or digging the garden. In years gone, by scrubbing the steps or hanging the mat on the washing line and giving it a good beating were very effective ways in which people were able to release tension and express their anger.

Punching pillows, pounding mattresses and beating the cushions of an armchair or a sofa can also be good ways of releasing anger. When using this method we would suggest that you kneel on the floor with your elbows resting on the chair or bed. We encourage you to speak out your feelings and express your anger. We didn't realize how much dust there can be in a chair cushion until we saw a young lady beating it as she got in touch with her buried anger about the abuse she had received!

Yet another way of releasing anger is to tear up an old telephone directory. You can rip out a page and then tear it in half again and again or screw the paper up and throw it on the floor. Don't worry about making a mess.

Initially we might help people by kneeling beside them in front of the sofa, speaking of our own anger at the way they were treated and the things that were said to them. We say we are angry at Satan because of all the hurt and pain that he has brought into their lives.

At the same time we begin to encourage them to speak out their own feelings. As we do this we are trying to help them express their emotions. This is not the same as some secular therapies in which people are encouraged to imagine that cushions or pillows are the people who have hurt them and to direct their anger against these substitutes. This may only fuel hatred against those who have hurt them, which is not helpful.

To move into healing, people need to get to a place where they are able to forgive those who have caused them pain. God doesn't want us to hate others, but we can hate the work of the enemy through them. We try to help the person direct their anger against the sins rather than the sinners. If they say things like, "I hate you, uncle," we would encourage them to say instead, "I hate what you made me do ..." or "I hate the words that you said that I was ..."

Releasing anger should not be seen as an end in itself but as part of the healing process. The anger is usually a secondary emotion sitting on top of hurt, rejection, guilt and shame. As the anger is released these other emotions often surface.

When Sheila came for help on a healing retreat she was forty. Her parents separated when she was four years old and her stepfather sexually abused her right up to her adult years. Because of this her mother hated her. We demonstrated how we can release anger by hitting a bed or a sofa. She wasn't able to do that but was able to tear up an old telephone book. We discovered that underneath the anger was a lot of grief and pain.

Emotional release

In ministry we encourage people who have been abused to express their emotions. We find it helpful to say out loud that what happened to them was not God's plan for their life. We speak out that we are sorry about what happened to them. We might say the following: "As a man, I want to say that I am sorry for what men have done to you," or "As a mother, I am sorry that your mother treated you this way."

Speaking such words can be very healing. It may be the first time that anyone has acknowledged that what happened to them was wrong. Often people who have been abused carry a deep inward desire that abusers would one day admit they did wrong, take responsibility for what happened and ask for forgiveness. People who have been abused as children sometimes tell us that at a certain age the abuse stopped and nothing else was ever spoken about it. The abuser treated them as if nothing had happened but they were left to struggle on through life devastated by the experience.

Maybe you will have a time of ministry when you can begin to release your emotional pain and hurt. Those ministering to you can be a channel of God's love and comfort. It might be appropriate for them to hold your hand or embrace you in their arms. You may be a person who doesn't feel comfortable with physical touch so it is very important that this is only done with your permission. You need to feel safe and secure and be in a place of trusting them.

Jane, who attended one of our healing retreats, wrote the following testimony:

> I have spent most of my life dominated by fear, anger and unable to relate properly to other people. I have had many types of counseling and ministry but nothing seemed to bring the necessary freedom or the real root cause. I was constantly struggling with anger, self-pity, rejection and the inability to really know God. I arrived apprehensive, bound up and angry, but God began to work from the first ministry session. Although the process was difficult and extremely painful I never once felt threatened or rejected. Because of this I was able to allow God to touch memories of sexual abuse that had been buried all my life. They were exposed, dealt with and healed.

Forgiveness

As emotional pain is released we encourage people to speak forgiveness towards those who have caused the hurt and pain. It might be for specific things that were said or done or things that were not done. The speaking of forgiveness often triggers a deeper level of emotional release. Forgiveness is difficult, and we will talk about it in the next chapter. Don't be in a hurry to rush on to the next step. When you truly forgive, you may find another layer of emotional pain which was buried, and which Jesus wants to share and heal. Those ministering to others should not be in a hurry either, and should allow plenty of time for any emotional release to take place.

As we minister and help people release their hurt and pain, we often remember the lady who came and wept over the feet of Jesus (Luke 7:36–50). The Bible says very little about this woman other than that she was known as a sinful woman and was probably, therefore, a prostitute. Whilst her tears may have been tears of repentance, there may have been much more than that behind these tears.

Perhaps for the first time in her life she had found someone she could trust and feel safe with. Perhaps for the first time in her life she was getting in touch with the hurt and pain that led her into the lifestyle she now led. Possibly, like many of the individuals that we have ministered to who have ended up in "sinful lifestyles," she had been a victim of sexual abuse and was beginning to release the associated pain. We don't know for sure, but we do know that Jesus treated this woman with great kindness and compassion.

Summary

Those who have suffered abuse need encouragement to express and release all the emotions of anger, hurt and pain. Such release will help to unravel the confusion they are feeling and is an important step in bringing peace to their turmoil and torment. If this applies to you, don't rush this important step.

In the next chapter we will look at all the steps involved in finding hope and healing after abuse.

Hope and Healing

10

We believe that it is God's desire to bring healing to every part of our being that has been affected by the abuse we may have experienced. In this chapter we are going to give you some key steps in moving forward into healing and wholeness. Not every step will be applicable in every situation, so it is important for you to be asking the Holy Spirit to guide you as you read and apply them in your own life.

Step 1 – Forgive those who have abused you in any way

Perhaps the most important single step in dealing with the abuse you have experienced is to forgive all those who have abused you in any way. This is not easy to do, but it is what Jesus asks us to do. Unless you forgive you will remain chained to the past and unable to move forward. Without forgiveness there is no lasting freedom.

Following her healing retreat Brenda wrote the following:

> I had a bad relationship with both my parents, and was abused as a child by my father. I always suffered rejection and as a result became a very closed person, unable to

trust anyone. Aggression and anger had been suppressed within. I also suffered from bouts of depression and sometimes contemplated suicide. In an act of my will I forgave those I needed to, including my parents. This began the emotional forgiveness process. All I can say is, "Praise God!" I'm more peaceful, I don't get aggressive and worked up any more, and I'm not depressed.

Forgiveness is not minimizing or condoning what was done to you. Forgiveness is not denying the feelings you have about what happened. It is OK to feel angry about what happened and to express that anger in a godly way. Forgiveness is not erasing or forgetting the past. It is not forgiving and forgetting. Rather, forgiveness is more like lancing a painful boil. It allows the poison to be released. There may still be a scar but not the severe pain.

Forgiveness does not mean that you have to trust the person who has hurt you. The person will have to earn that trust. It does not mean that you have to go back into a place where you will receive further abuse. Forgiveness is not pardoning a person and saying that their sin against me is no longer punishable. Only God can pardon someone in that sense. When God forgives us, He is not saying that the sin is not punishable but rather that Jesus has Himself taken the punishment for the sin.

Forgiveness of others means granting a person more mercy than they deserve, just as Jesus has shown us more mercy than we deserve. Forgiveness means dismissing bitterness and resentment from your heart. Forgiveness means giving up your desire for revenge and retaliation. When we are hurt, our carnal nature wants us to get our own back – to inflict punishment on the person who has hurt us. We want to judge the person and execute the sentence upon them.

Forgiveness, however, means releasing the person from your judgment as to what the penalty should be. It is like handing the case to a higher authority to deal with. When you release someone into the freedom of your forgiveness you are handing them over to God. We do this in the knowledge that God will deal with the person in a just and righteous way.

You need to recognize that forgiveness starts in the will. It is a choice that you make. You might not feel like forgiving but you choose to line up your will with God's will for your life. Forgiveness comes out of a heart attitude that wants to be right with God. Making this choice to forgive allows the healing process to start.

When you forgive you need to try to separate the sin from the sinner. This will help you to direct your anger against what was done to you rather than against the person who did it. We are not trying to excuse the person for what they did but this distinction will help you to deal with your heart response to what happened.

I (Liz) was once in a country overseas where I didn't speak the language and at the end of a teaching session a man came up to me and asked if I would pray with his wife. She had only half an hour and then had to leave the conference to return home. As I listened to the story of her life, I wondered what could possibly be said or done to help her in such a short time.

She had experienced childhood sexual abuse which had ruined her life and resulted in years of therapy but no progress towards healing. She felt unable to work, go out shopping or visit her church. She had heard Christians talk about the need to forgive but said she was totally unable to do so. I shared that forgiving is not condoning what was done to us or saying it wasn't wrong, but that it was handing over all judgment of sin to God.

The lady suddenly said, "Well, now you have explained this to me I can forgive my abuser." She did so, and as I asked God to pour in His love and comfort to the part of her which had suffered all the abuse the tears began to roll down her cheeks. She was quite overawed because she had not expressed any emotion for years and years. All her feelings had been frozen.

Her husband said he and the friends at the house group would be more than willing to pray further into her healing.

You may need to ask Jesus to help you to forgive. In our human nature we don't want to forgive. We need to ask Jesus for His heart of forgiveness. We need some of the forgiveness that Jesus had that enabled Him to pray, "Father, forgive them for they know not what they do." Ask Jesus to help you see the person as Jesus sees them – a sinner worth dying for. You can speak out your forgiveness in a prayer such as this:

> **Thank You, Jesus, for dying that I might be forgiven. By an act of my will I now choose to forgive those who have hurt me or abused me in any way. I choose to forgive** _____ [at this point you should name the individuals out loud]. **I release each and every one of these people into the freedom of my forgiveness. In Jesus' Name. Amen.**

Forgiveness is a process, and we encourage you to keep choosing to walk in that forgiveness. Each time you remember the pain or injustice that you experienced, you need to continue to choose to forgive the people involved.

Step 2 – Forgive those who should have protected you from abuse

When we have been abused we need to forgive those who should have protected us from being abused. We might need to forgive the mother who turned a blind eye even though she suspected that her husband or a new partner might be behaving inappropriately towards her daughter. It might be the social worker who failed to observe and report the signs of physical abuse, maltreatment or neglect in the foster home. It might be the teacher who didn't deal with the incidents of bullying when we were at school. It might be the police or the judicial system that somehow minimalized the offence and sins against us and left us feeling that we had not received the justice we deserved.

We can speak out our forgiveness in a prayer such as this:

> **Lord Jesus, by an act of my will I now choose to forgive those who failed to protect me from being abused. I choose to forgive** _____ [at this point you should name the individuals out loud and verbalize what you are forgiving them for]. **I release each and every one of these people into the freedom of my forgiveness. In Jesus' Name. Amen.**

Step 3 – Repent of any ungodly response that you have made out of your hurt and pain

No matter what others have done to us we need to respond in godly ways. This does not mean that we shouldn't judge their actions and agree with God that we have been sinned against and feel angry about that. It does mean, however, that our response should be godly. If we have responded in an ungodly way we need to confess and repent. To confess means to agree with God's verdict on what we have done. It is taking responsibility for what we have done without blaming others.

To repent means to turn away from the things that we did that were wrong. It is telling God that if the same circumstances arose we would not want to respond in the same way. If a woman still smiles and gets satisfaction out of having damaged her husband's car, when she discovered he was having an affair behind her back, or says, "I would do the same again if I discovered my spouse cheating on me," she hasn't reached that place of true repentance.

It is reality that in the same circumstances she might still feel like damaging his car or worse. However, true repentance is getting to a place where she can say that she will ignore such feelings and desires for retaliation but instead will exercise her freedom of choice to do what is godly rather than what is ungodly.

The following prayer can be used as a basis for bringing these issues before God:

> **Father, I confess that as a result of being hurt I have allowed myself to sin by** _____ [be specific and name ungodly attitudes, thinking patterns and behavior]. **I acknowledge my sin and I now repent and turn from it, asking that You will forgive me and cleanse me. In Jesus' Name. Amen.**

Step 4 – Ask God to forgive you for blaming Him for the abuse you have suffered

If we have blamed God for what has happened in our lives and been angry with God, we need to recognize our wrongdoing in this. God loves us and wants the best for us. We may not understand all that happens to us but we need to get angry with the enemy of our soul, who delights in the bad things that happen to us, rather than blame God.

Take a moment to consider whether you have been angry with God and blamed Him for things that Satan or other people have done. This type of prayer may help:

> **Please forgive me, Lord, for blaming You for what others have done to me. I know that You hate what Satan has done in my life. Thank You for loving me and promising to set me free. Amen.**

Step 5 – Repentance for rejecting self

Maybe as a consequence of being hurt and abused by others, you have internalized your anger against yourself. You may have done this by self-harming or by contemplating or attempting suicide. Such thoughts and actions are ultimately a rejection of who you are. It is a rejection of God's gift of life to you. It is a rejection of yourself as a valued and precious creation of God.

Such self-rejection is agreeing with the purposes and plans that Satan has for your life. His objectives are to steal and destroy. When we reject ourselves and God's gift of life we are giving the enemy rights in our life. If we have done these things we need to bring them before the Lord in confession and repentance. You can do this with a prayer such as:

> **Thank You, Father, for my life and for creating me as me. Thank You, Jesus, that You love me so much that You died in order that I might have life. I now repent of wanting to die and renounce the contract I made with Satan by wishing I were dead. I now choose life and take away from Satan every right to my life that I gave him by my attitudes or desires. I now choose to live for Jesus and make Him Lord of every area of my life. In Jesus' name. Amen.**

Step 6 – Inner healing and godly expression of emotions

When there has been abuse there will almost certainly be unexpressed emotions and anger. Sometimes these emotions have been denied and pushed down. Often the victim of abuse has been threatened or punished for expressing emotions or felt guilty about having feelings about the abuse.

In Chapter 9 we looked at ways in which we can express our emotions and anger in godly ways. It is often appropriate to do this as part of the healing process. It is good sometimes to speak out a prayer giving God permission to bring release and healing to our emotions.

We find that during ministry people need to be encouraged not to be fearful but trust that Jesus will help them face and deal with their emotions in a way that they are able to cope with. The following prayer is a good one, if you recognize that you may have denied or buried your emotions and need to submit your healing to Jesus:

Father God, I thank You for my emotions.

I confess that I have not always recognized or fully accepted my emotions or properly understood their place in how You made me.

I confess that I have not expressed my emotions correctly – I have pushed them down, ignored them, or allowed them uncontrolled reign. As a result I have caused hurt to myself and others. Please forgive me for doing this.

I confess that I have sometimes used my emotions and my anger in ungodly ways and sought to control and manipulate others through my emotional behavior. I repent of doing this and ask You to forgive me.

I ask You now, Father to help me express my emotions and buried feelings in godly ways. I choose to face the hurt and pain and give You permission to bring Your healing into these areas of my life.

I ask these things in the name of my Lord Jesus. Amen.

After having prayed this prayer, allow God to put you in touch with releasing your hurt, pain and anger.

For some people this step will be the most important part of moving forward. For some there will be a need to express some of the well of emotional pain before they can forgive. In the midst of facing and expressing the pain we need to continue to speak out forgiveness of those who have hurt us.

Step 7 – Breaking of ungodly ties

Every kind of abuse results in the establishment of an ungodly soul-tie between the abuser and their victim. Relationship bonds, instead of being a channel of blessing, have become a channel of cursing and need to be dealt with.

After having chosen to forgive those who have abused us in any way, there is a need to break any ungodly ties that have been formed. A prayer such as the following can be used:

> **I proclaim a breaking of the ungodly tie existing between me and _____ [name the individuals]. I ask You, God, to sever that linking and completely separate out and restore to me every part of myself which has been wrongfully tied to _____ [name the individuals]. I ask You to return to them any part of their being which has wrongfully been tied to me. I ask this in Jesus' name. Amen.**

Sometimes in ministry as we pray this prayer we see spontaneous deliverance taking place. Sometimes emotional release will take place. There might even be a mixture of both so we need to be asking God for discernment and His guidance as to how to pray.

Step 8 – Deliverance

Where the enemy has been given rights in our lives as a result of our sins against others, or the sins of others affecting us (including those of our ancestors), there may be a need for deliverance. Before attempting deliverance it is important that the enemy's rights to be there are taken away through confession, repentance and renunciation of sin, and forgiveness of those who have sinned against us.

Because demons latch into and feed off emotional pain, it is usually a good idea to bind up the demons first and deal with the healing of inner pain and expressing the emotion of anger in a godly way. Afterwards we can cast out the demons.

Where inner healing issues have not been dealt with first, strong manifestations and violent outbursts that are difficult to control may interfere with any attempts at deliverance. On the other hand, after dealing with the inner healing issues we usually find that deliverance is a very quiet and easy experience. It may be that the person yawns, coughs or gives a deep sigh as demons are commanded to go.

Tessa was a lady who had been abused by her brother at the age of seven. Sadly her mother became ill with cancer a year later. All through her childhood she had had no real protection or proper nurture. As deliverance was attempted there was quite a bit of difficulty with demons shouting out, "You can't have her, she's mine."

The ministry team began praying for Jesus to minister to the feelings she had at the age of seven. As she put her head on the knee of one of the ladies in the team, the team began softly singing "Jesus, Jesus, holy and anointed One, Jesus." After she had received love and peace from the Lord it became easy to take authority over the demons and cast them out.

Although freedom from demonic bondage can be achieved through self-deliverance, we would generally recommend that you ask someone with understanding and experience in this area to pray with you as other issues may surface during the ministry.

We remember praying with Sylvia who came on a healing retreat seeking help for the abuse she had suffered as a small girl. She was much neglected as a child and as she got in touch with her emotions she began crying. As we prayed for deliverance she experienced sharp pains in her body, but as we took authority over the evil spirits and told them to leave Sylvia felt those pains disappear as quickly as they had appeared.

Sylvia not only had a deliverance need in her life but, more importantly, she also needed to know the love of her heavenly Father. With Sylvia's permission, the man who was part of the ministry team became a kind of daddy substitute just for a few minutes allowing Sylvia to cuddle up close to him. He was able to model the safe father's love that she never experienced or received as a child and become a channel of God's love to Sylvia.

During ministry, people receiving deliverance need to be encouraged to exercise their will and authority in telling the enemy to leave. The evil spirits can be addressed in the following way:

> **In the name of Jesus I command every unclean spirit** [or alternatively **the spirit of** _____ (name the area of bondage)] **to leave** _____ [name the person] **without hurting or harming them or any other person and without going into any other member of their family. In Jesus' Name. Amen.**

When helping someone who has been abused, areas of demonic bondage that need to be addressed may include some or all of the following:

- spirits of domination and control (from the abuser)
- spirits of rejection, self-rejection and fear of rejection
- unclean sexual spirits (incubus and succubus spirits, spirits of perversion, homosexuality or bestiality, etc.)
- spirits of abuse
- spirits of confusion, condemnation and false guilt
- spirits of unforgiveness, bitterness, suicide and death wish (often the reaction to the abuse will have given rights to these spirits)
- spirits of infirmity and death
- spirits of passivity and a victim spirit.

The actual words used in addressing any demonic bondage are relatively unimportant. The important thing is to know (and exercise) the authority that we have in Jesus to deal with the enemy, once his rights to be there have been removed.

As the demonic is addressed there may be manifestations such as coughing or deep yawning. Sometimes there may be no visible manifestations. As deliverance is ministered it is important that people do not remain passive and indifferent to what is going on. They need to recognize their own authority over the strongholds that the enemy has established in their lives. The person ministering should encourage them to be agreeing in their mind and spirit with the deliverance prayers and agreeing with the command for the demonic to go.

Following deliverance we would ask God to fill the person afresh with His Holy Spirit. We would ask God to continue His work of healing and cleansing and to bring His peace into their life. As in the case of Sylvia above, there may be a need for some further inner healing following deliverance. The person ministering needs to be sensitive to the leading of the Holy Spirit. We will ask people what they sense is happening. Some may sense that there is still something that needs to be addressed. Others will know they have been released and will be full of thanks and joy for their new freedom.

Summary

In this chapter we have outlined the important key steps to healing from abuse. At Ellel Ministries the ministry team has had the privilege of seeing many, many people set free from the consequences of abuse as these key principles have been applied.

In the last chapter of this book we will look at steps to moving on into the plans that God has for your life.

Free to Live

In this final chapter of the book we want to encourage you to move forward into the plans and purposes that God has for your life. As we deal with the chains holding us to the past we become free to enter into God's future for us.

We wrote earlier about Jesus' heart to bring healing to the abused as expressed in the book of Isaiah:

> The Spirit of the Sovereign LORD is on me,
>   because the LORD has anointed me
>   to preach good news to the poor.
> He has sent me to bind up the broken-hearted,
>   to proclaim freedom for the captives
>   and release from darkness for the prisoners,
> to proclaim the year of the LORD's favour
>   and the day of vengeance of our God,
> to comfort all who mourn,
>   and provide for those who grieve in Zion –
> to bestow on them a crown of beauty
>   instead of ashes,
> the oil of gladness
>   instead of mourning,
> and a garment of praise
>   instead of a spirit of despair.   (Isaiah 61:1–3a)

These verses speak about healing and being set free from captivity. The next two verses are, we believe, very encouraging to all those who have suffered and need healing:

> They will be called oaks of righteousness,
>   a planting of the LORD
>   for the display of his splendour.
> They will rebuild the ancient ruins
>   and restore the places long devastated;
> they will renew the ruined cities
>   that have been devastated for generations.
>
> (Isaiah 61:3b–4)

These verses firstly talk about the damaged and broken-hearted becoming people that reflect the splendor of God. If you have experienced abuse, take hope from this promise of God. God can take that which has been damaged and broken and restore it to something of great splendor. God could do this for you too. It is our great privilege and joy to meet so many who come for help, bowed down with shame and deep self-rejection, and receive real healing from Jesus. As Jesus does His work of healing in them, radiance comes into their whole being and they go out with their heads held upright knowing their security and true value in Jesus. We know He would delight to do the same for you too.

The promises of God for you

For many the abuse in their lives has resulted in devastation but these verses talk about the rebuilding of that which has been devastated. Note that the ones who do the rebuilding are the ones that were damaged but who now have been healed. As you seek to rebuild your life, draw strength from the promises of God for you. In the appendix we have included some encouraging and helpful scriptures for you to meditate upon. Allow God to speak to you through them. Use them to counter the negativity and lies that the enemy would whisper into your ears.

If you are not in a church we encourage you to find one that can be your spiritual home and provide ongoing help and support. This might seem a difficult step for you. Because you have been let down and betrayed you may find it difficult to put your trust in anyone who is in authority. You may have withdrawn or isolated yourself out of fear of further rejection or abuse.

However, as we receive our healing and we learn to put our trust in Jesus we can feel safer to open up to others. If they reject us we can take the hurt to Jesus knowing that He will receive us. We can encourage ourselves through the wonderful promise of Psalm 27:10:

> *Though my father and mother forsake me,*
> *the* LORD *will receive me.*

We encourage you to take rightful control over your life. Become the driver of your own life with Jesus as the navigator. Learn to exercise your free will and make godly choices. Choose to do things because you want to please others, not because you are fearful of their rejecting you. Say "no" when it is appropriate. Set boundaries and establish priorities for your life. Set realistic short- and long-term goals – objectives that are achievable so that your self-esteem is built up as you achieve these goals.

Centrality of praise and worship

We encourage you to make praise and worship a part of your life. We can enter into the presence of God through praise and worship (Psalm 100). When you feel down and think the way forward is difficult, choose to worship the God of all creation.

Put on some praise and worship music and choose to focus on God.

Paul and Silas were unjustly abused and imprisoned. They could have chosen to grumble and complain and to go into self-pity but they didn't. Instead freedom came to them as they entered into worship (Acts 16:22–26).

Many times we have seen how singing anointed worship songs about God's Father heart have helped damaged and wounded individuals. In the midst of the praise and worship they start to sob. As the emotional pain surfaces God begins to put in His truth and love. The next day we often hear testimony about how this was the first time people realized at a heart level that God loved and cared for them.

Keep your eyes on Jesus

No matter where you are in your walk to wholeness we encourage you to keep your eyes upon Jesus – the One who was so shamefully abused that you might have life as well as hope and healing.

You may like to pray the following prayer:

Lord Jesus, I thank You that You can identify with the pain and hurt that I have received through abuse. Thank You, Lord Jesus, that through the cross You have made provision for my healing. I thank You that You will complete Your work of healing in my life so that I can become a planting of the Lord for a display of Your splendor.

Appendix – Scriptures to Encourage

We find the scriptures below helpful when ministering hope and healing to the victims of abuse. Read them and meditate on the truths contained within them and allow God's Holy Spirit to touch you with His healing power.

Psalm 3:1–6

> O LORD, how many are my foes!
>   How many rise up against me!
> Many are saying of me,
>   "God will not deliver him."
> But you are a shield around me, O LORD;
>   you bestow glory on me and lift up my head.
> To the LORD I cry aloud,
>   and he answers me from his holy hill.
> I lie down and sleep;
>   I wake again, because the LORD sustains me.
> I will not fear the tens of thousands
>   drawn up against me on every side.

Psalm 8:3–6

> When I consider your heavens,
>   the work of your fingers,

the moon and the stars,
which you have set in place,
what is man that you are mindful of him,
the son of man that you care for him?
You made him a little lower than the heavenly beings
and crowned him with glory and honour.
You made him ruler over the works of your hands;
you put everything under his feet.

Psalm 34:17–18

The righteous cry out, and the LORD hears them;
he delivers them from all their troubles.
The LORD is close to the broken-hearted
and saves those who are crushed in spirit.

Psalm 68:4–6

Sing to God, sing praise to his name,
extol him who rides on the clouds –
his name is the LORD –
and rejoice before him.
A father to the fatherless, a defender of widows,
is God in his holy dwelling.
God sets the lonely in families;
he leads forth the prisoners with singing . . .

Psalm 139:13–16

For you created my inmost being;
you knit me together in my mother's womb.
I praise you because I am fearfully and
wonderfully made;
your works are wonderful,
I know that full well.

My frame was not hidden from you
  when I was made in the secret place.
When I was woven together in the depths
    of the earth,
  your eyes saw my unformed body.
All the days ordained for me
  were written in your book
  before one of them came to be.

Psalm 145:8–9

The LORD is gracious and compassionate,
  slow to anger and rich in love.
The LORD is good to all;
  he has compassion on all he has made.

Isaiah 40:10–11

See, the Sovereign LORD comes with power,
  and his arm rules for him.
See, his reward is with him,
  and his recompense accompanies him.
He tends his flock like a shepherd:
  He gathers the lambs in his arms
and carries them close to his heart;
  he gently leads those that have young.

Isaiah 40:29–31

He gives strength to the weary
  and increases the power of the weak.
Even youths grow tired and weary,
  and young men stumble and fall;
but those who hope in the LORD
  will renew their strength.

They will soar on wings like eagles;
    they will run and not grow weary,
    they will walk and not be faint.

Isaiah 43:1–4

But now, this is what the LORD says –
    he who created you, O Jacob,
    he who formed you, O Israel:
"Fear not, for I have redeemed you;
    I have summoned you by name;
        you are mine.
When you pass through the waters,
    I will be with you;
and when you pass through the rivers,
    they will not sweep over you.
When you walk through the fire,
    you will not be burned;
    the flames will not set you ablaze.
For I am the LORD, your God,
    the Holy One of Israel, your Saviour;
I give Egypt for your ransom,
    Cush and Seba in your stead.
Since you are precious and honoured
        in my sight,
    and because I love you,
I will give men in exchange for you,
    and people in exchange for your life.

Isaiah 61:1–3

The Spirit of the Sovereign LORD is on me,
    because the LORD has anointed me
    to preach good news to the poor.
He has sent me to bind up the broken-hearted,

to proclaim freedom for the captives
and release from darkness for the prisoners,
to proclaim the year of the LORD's favour
and the day of vengeance of our God,
to comfort all who mourn,
and provide for those who grieve in Zion –
to bestow on them a crown of beauty
instead of ashes,
the oil of gladness
instead of mourning,
and a garment of praise
instead of a spirit of despair.
They will be called oaks of righteousness,
a planting of the LORD
for the display of his splendour.

Isaiah 62:2–5

The nations will see your righteousness,
and all kings your glory;
you will be called by a new name
that the mouth of the LORD will bestow.
You will be a crown of splendour in the
LORD's hand,
a royal diadem in the hand of your God.
No longer will they call you Deserted,
or name your land Desolate.
But you will be called Hephzibah,
and your land Beulah;
for the LORD will take delight in you,
and your land will be married.
As a young man marries a maiden,
so will your sons marry you;
as a bridegroom rejoices over his bride,
so will your God rejoice over you.

Jeremiah 29:11

"For I know the plans I have for you," declares the LORD, "plans to prosper you and not to harm you, plans to give you hope and a future."

Zephaniah 3:17

"The LORD your God is with you,
he is mighty to save.
He will take great delight in you,
he will quiet you with his love,
he will rejoice over you with singing."

Matthew 11:28–30

"Come to me, all you who are weary and burdened, and I will give you rest. Take my yoke upon you and learn from me, for I am gentle and humble in heart, and you will find rest for your souls. For my yoke is easy and my burden is light."

John 8:31–32

To the Jews who had believed him, Jesus said, "If you hold to my teaching, you are really my disciples. Then you will know the truth, and the truth will set you free."

John 10:10–11

"The thief comes only to steal and kill and destroy; I have come that they may have life, and have it to the full. I am the good shepherd. The good shepherd lays down his life for the sheep.'

John 14:27

"Peace I leave with you; my peace I give you. I do not give to you as the world gives. Do not let your hearts be troubled and do not be afraid."

Romans 8:1–2

Therefore, there is now no condemnation for those who are in Christ Jesus, because through Christ Jesus the law of the Spirit of life set me free from the law of sin and death.

Romans 8:35, 37–38

Who shall separate us from the love of Christ? Shall trouble or hardship or persecution or famine or nakedness or danger or sword? . . . No, in all these things we are more than conquerors through him who loved us. For I am convinced that neither death nor life, neither angels nor demons, neither the present nor the future, nor any powers, neither height nor depth, nor anything else in all creation, will be able to separate us from the love of God that is in Christ Jesus our Lord.

Revelation 3:20

"Behold I stand at the door and knock. If anyone hears My voice and opens the door, I will come in to him and dine with him, and he with Me."   (NKJV)

Sovereign World Ltd
&
Ellel Ministries International

In a stroke of divine master planning both Sovereign World and Ellel Ministries were independently founded in the same year – 1986.

Sovereign World, founded by Chris Mungeam, has become a widely respected Christian publishing imprint and Ellel Ministries, founded by Peter Horrobin, has developed a world-wide network of Centres, each designed to resource and equip the Church through healing retreats, courses and training schools.

Twenty years later, in April 2006, Ellel Ministries purchased Sovereign World Ltd to continue the precious work of publishing outstanding Christian teaching, as well as to create a publishing arm for Ellel Ministries. It was a divine knitting together of these two organizations both of which share the vision to proclaim the Kingdom of God by preaching the good news, healing the broken-hearted and setting the captives free.

If you would like to know more about Ellel Ministries their UK contact information is:

International Headquarters
Ellel Grange
Ellel
Lancaster
LA2 0HN
UK

Tel: +44 (0)1524 751651
Fax: +44 (0)1524 751738
Email: info.grange@ellelministries.org

For details of other Centres please refer to the website at:
www.ellelministries.org

Anger is the most powerful of emotions. It can be the driving force that enables us to achieve the seemingly impossible or the stumbling block that traps us into a life style characterized by unforgiveness, bitterness, broken relationships and violence. Keys presented in this book will explain how you can deal with the accumulation of anger from past events and how you can in future deal with the situations that cause you to feel angry. The book also provides much needed understanding for those in the caring ministries who are seeking to help those with 'an anger problem'.

Anger: How Do You Handle It? *by Paul & Liz Giffin*
£6.99 | 978-185240-4505 | 112pp | Sovereign World Ltd

Whilst the Church's standards in sexual matters may be higher than those of the world they are often still nowhere near God's standards. We live in a world that has distorted the godly concept of sexuality. As a result there are many Christians living in guilt or struggling because of a lack of knowledge, wrong past choices or as a consequence of sins that others have committed against them. The driving force behind the ungodly expression of our sexuality is a seeking after false love and acceptence. The author brilliantly exposes the lies of the enemy, which can trap us into ungodly sexual practices.

Sex: God's Truth *by Jill Southern*
£6.99 | 978-185240-4529 | 128pp | Sovereign World Ltd

When we realize that relationships are more than just a physical meeting of two people, we begin to understand that some of our relationships might have affected our lives in a negative way. We may find ourselves damaged and tied in a place of bondage from which God wants us to be set free. A way of describing this unseen hold that ties us to bad relationships is an ungodly soul-tie. It is a tie in the spiritual realm that has a hold on the soul. As you read this book you will discover how to find release from ungody soul-ties and most impotantly experience God's freedom and healing.

Soul Ties: The Unseen Bond in Relationships *by David Cross*
£6.99 | 978-185240-4512 | 128pp | Sovereign World Ltd

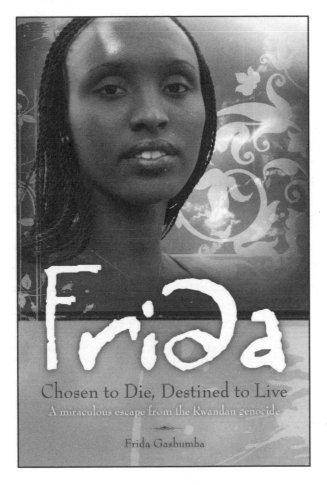

Frida witnessed her family being massacred by Hutu men with machetes and was then asked how she wanted to die. She could not afford a bullet, which they offered to sell her, so instead received what should have been a fatal blow to the head. She was put in a mass grave with her slaughtered family only to find herself still alive and conscious. She eventually climbed out of the pit covered in filth and blood. Remarkably, Frida's message is one of immense hope and personal deliverance pointing towards the transforming power of forgiveness. This book tells the true, dramatic story of life amid the horror of genocide and her miraculous escape.

Frida: Chosen to Die, Destined to Live *by Frida Gashumba*
£8.99 | 978-185240-4758 | 176pp | Sovereign World Ltd

We hope you enjoyed reading this Sovereign World book.
For more details of other Sovereign books and
new releases see our website:

www.sovereignworld.com

If you would like to help us send a copy of this book
and many other titles to needy pastors in developing
countries, please write for further information
or send your gift to:

**Sovereign World Trust
PO Box 777
Tonbridge, Kent TN11 0ZS
United Kingdom**

You can also visit **www.sovereignworldtrust.com**.
The Trust is a registered charity.